Books by Paul Dickson

The Great American Ice Cream Book   (*1972*)

Think Tanks   (*1971*)

The Great American
Ice Cream Book

The
Great American
ICE CREAM
Book

PAUL DICKSON

Atheneum · New York

1972

The only emperor is the emperor of ice cream.
                                    WALLACE STEVENS

This book is dedicated both to those central heroes and heroines who appear in it—like the infamous "Two Quart" Butler, the innovative Nancy Johnson, and the apostolic John Matthews—and to those who for reasons of space did not fit into the narrative that follows. Among the stalwarts of the latter group that must be mentioned are:

"EMPEROR" J. ACKERMAN COLES, who left a trust fund to the town of Scotch Plains, New Jersey, for the sole purpose of treating its children to free ice cream once a year.

"EMPEROR" ALBERT S. PACETTA, who, as New York Markets Commissioner during the administration of Mayor Robert Wagner, upheld the right of the New Yorker to purchase one ice cream scoop instead of two, thereby thwarting vendors who insisted that he had to buy two.

"EMPEROR" JOHN BERTOLINI of Corona, Queens, one of the world's last practicing ice cream sculptors, who has selflessly watched over 100,000 of his works—including busts of Queen Elizabeth and Richard Nixon—being eaten.

"EMPRESS" NANCY, who helped me keep my research materials from melting, by eating half of them with me.

Contents

I *Renaissance*

STREET SCENE	*3*
THE CREAMING OF AMERICA	*8*
THE ENDLESS SUMMER OF '72, '73, '74 . . .	*12*

II *Up from the Ice Age*

OLD WORLD EVOLUTION	*15*
ICE CREAM COMES TO THE NEW WORLD	*20*

III *The Annals of American Ice Cream (1851–1941)*

SUCCESS À LA MODE	*29*
THE UNCRANKING OF A GIANT	*31*
THE BUBBLE MELTS	*38*

IV *Ice Cream and the Modern Era (1941–1971)*

SYMBOL IN A SCOOP	*46*
THE GREAT ICE CREAM ORGY OF 1946	*50*
SUBVERSION OF THE SODA FOUNTAIN	*53*
DOMESTIC COLD WAR	*57*

Contents

V Frozen Assets—The Institutions of Ice Cream

Mr. Green's Expedient Soda 61

The Seventh-Day Concoction 64

The Somewhat Confusing Saga of the Ice Cream Cone 66

The Sticky Triumvirate 73

VI Jerks and Bubble Merchants

The Fountain's Youth 87

A Marble to Behold 92

Lament for the Soda Jerk 96

Thus He Spoke 99

VII The Anatomy of Ice Cream

Ice Cream Today 109

Just and Unjust Desserts 112

The Artful Technicians of Flavor 120

VIII Making It—A Basic Course in Ice Cream Construction

Cranking Out a Good Vanilla 128

Flavoring Seminar 134

Sherbets and Ices 141

Syrups and Toppings 144

IX An Annotated, Chronological Compendium of Concoctions, Constructions, and Conceits—Good Eats!

148

Appendix: What Obtains—A Buyer's Guide to Ice Cream Needs and Equipment 190

Index

The Great American
Ice Cream Book

I

Renaissance

Any minor interruptions to the Great Depression of the Spirit now upon the land are worthy of attention for no other reason than that they divert us from the mess at hand and offer us a chance to enter realms at once uplifting, comprehendible, and determinedly irrelevant in this age of relevance. No further apology is needed for concerning ourselves with the ongoing American ice cream revival.

STREET SCENE

Wall Street was awash with ice cream and the hottest rumors heard there concerned "free sprinkles" and "outasight maple walnut.'' One large vendor claimed to be dipping a cone a second in the area. Further uptown some of the nation's highest-paid executive talents spilled out of their glass and concrete lairs onto the streets to demand their chocolate, vanilla, and strawberry in ''sugar cones''—a delicacy previously known only to the *cognoscenti* that drew on a weekly allowance rather than a corporate expense account. Across town and into outer boroughs and suburbs, long lines appeared in front of signs marked Barricini, Barton's, Fannie Farmer, Chock Full o' Nuts, and Howard Johnson's. Meanwhile relief was on its way from the hinterland: H. P. Hood and Sons of Boston was sending a fleet of six hundred ice cream vending trucks to the city to supplement the beleaguered forces of Mister Softee and Good Humor; Baskin-Robbins was completing its march from the West Coast and was about to take New York; and dipping equipment and ice cream were being moved into locations ranging from twenty-seven new Yum Yums to nine established Zum Zums. Established parlors like Hicks and The Flick were more popular than ever, and their proprietors were keeping a competitive eye on the dozens of new independent parlors under construction. A turn-of-the-century parlor was discovered intact in Haverstraw, New York, and, with the painstaking care normally associated with archeological excavation, was being taken apart, packed up, and removed to Third Avenue to emerge as Agora. Reliable sources told of marble countertops being designed into an ice cream parlor which was to be located in the staid lobby of the Plaza Hotel. Summing it all up, Gael Greene wrote in a *New York* magazine cover story on ice cream in August, 1970: ''New York is in the full throes of an ice cream renaissance.''

Library of Congress
Typical turn-of-the-century pharmacy replete with soda fountain and soda jerk. This particular establishment is the Collins Pharmacy in Islip, Long Island.

Soon the New York *Times* was researching the phenomenon and *Look* had photographers on the streets capturing it in color.

While it was manifested most dramatically in New York, where it started during the summer of 1970 and continued to flourish through 1971 and into 1972, it was hitting all over the country as well. It is hard to determine exactly where it began, but cities ranging from Boston to San Francisco had seen earlier evidence of revived interest in high-quality ice cream, sparked by a variety of catalysts. Nationally, the movement of forces like Bresler's and Baskin-Robbins was significant—and then there were the local sparks. In New York, for example, people attribute great influence to the decision of the Barricini chain to bolster lagging candy sales by installing dipping counters. In San Francisco the steady parade of flavors coming out of the area's 31-store Swensen's chain and the must-be-seen-to-be-believed Ghirardelli Soda Fountain in Ghirardelli Square were of great importance, while in Boston most believe it was prompted by a combination of established entities—such as the remarkable Bailey's and Cabot's fountains—and new emphases: for one, Howard Johnson's was using its Boston-area stores to experiment with the long-overdue idea of again giving star billing to its fine ice cream rather than such things as its less-than-mediocre egg salad sandwiches. Nor was all of this restricted to urban and suburban America. There were also expanding pockets of rural excellence, such as Miller's ice cream parlors in Michigan and the Deering chain moving across Maine and into New Hampshire.

Lest there be any confusion about this ongoing revival, it has thus far had no significant impact on the quantity of ice

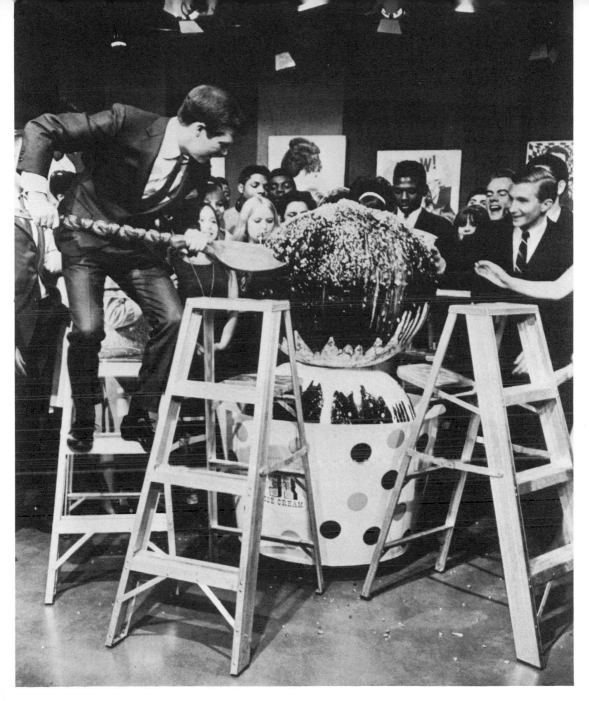

Baskin-Robbins
World's largest sundae, made by Baskin-Robbins Ice Cream on a Los Angeles television show and documented in the *Guinness Book of World Records.* The record has since been challenged.

cream being sold; today the average American consumes about the same amount of the stuff as he or she has every year since 1950. The revolution taking place is subjectively measured in terms of flavors tested, respect accorded, consumer behavior (meaning that ice cream cones were to be found clutched in the hands of an increasing number of adults, as anyone walking down any major urban street during the last few summers could see), and, most important, quality demanded. Children of all ages have begun to opt for good ice cream over that miracle of chemical engineering and technical expertise that has been passing for ice cream for so long. Despite the much-publicized contemporary worry about the dollar and the calorie, droves of Americans are deserting the anemic 69-cent half-gallon for a 35-cent double-scoop of rich, full-bodied, fattening ice cream.

THE CREAMING OF AMERICA

Added to these delightful goings-on were all the attempts to explain the sudden adult rediscovery of quality ice cream. Opined *The Nation's Restaurant News:* "Behind the change in consumer consciousness lies the youth culture, nostalgia and recessionary economics." The trade biweekly backed up its assessment with quotes gathered from restaurant owners and ice cream eaters across the country, which alluded to such specifics as "rebellion against the machine culture," the demise of "phony sophistication," "sensual pleasure," and a "desire for the good old days." *Look,* in one of its last ventures into pop psychology, tried to explain the sudden addiction this way:

"Perhaps it's nothing more complicated than mother's milk—in 28 flavors, and you get to choose." William Holmes, Atlantic Coast manager for Beatrice Foods (a combine which owns a diverse stable of ice cream labels, including the prestigious Louis Sherry brand), says: "There is something about hard times that brings out an urge for simple pleasures like ice cream." He adds, with the trained eye of an ice cream marketer: "Of course, there is a very simple thing at work here too. Long ago, ice cream left downtown for the shopping mall and supermarket and now it's back. A lot of people never ate ice cream cones on their lunch hour simply because they couldn't get them." Said Gael Greene in *New York* magazine: "In these harsh and uncertain times, as the establishment cracks and institutions crumble, it is no wonder we reach out to ice cream. It is a link to innocence and security, healing, soothing, wholesome. . . ." Spotting the same urge elsewhere, *Metro Boston* called it "a relief from reality, a throwback to the childhood and a less complex world." *Business Week*'s predictable emphasis was on "a tremendous proliferation of specialty shops, flavors and some shrewd marketing." And to the New York *Times* it was all attributable to a new "era of informality."

Everyone was getting into the act, including those who pushed beyond analysis to application. In *The Sensuous Woman,* J. rhapsodized on the sensuous qualities of ice cream, going so far as to outline a cone-lapping exercise for raising sensual consciousness. Dr. David Reuben, author of *Everything You Always Wanted to Know about Sex but Were Afraid to Ask,* in one of the most rampantly simplistic articles to appear on sex since the 1950s, when Pat Boone gave advice on such matters, told *Woman's Day* readers in 1971 that the sure-fire way of nailing a man was to serve him milk, cream, or ice cream. Reuben, presumably on a grant from the National Dairy Council, unflinchingly offered this as his keystone theory to the man/woman relationship:

> For every man the world of the subconscious is ruled by the symbol of milk. Milk shakes, ice cream, even alcoholic beverages . . . carry the theme of Mother's milk throughout every day. The six-foot, two-hundred pound man sipping a cup of coffee with cream is emotionally only moments away from the ten-pound baby happily drinking from his bottle. . . . When a woman establishes herself as the *provider of milk* she literally makes herself part of her man's unconscious mind. If she wants him to marry her, all she has to do is inject enough milk (or milk substitute) into their relationship.

Enjoying this profundity and analysis most were those of us who had *actually* got the whole thing going. We were the ones who had sought out, supported, and freely advertised high-quality ice cream when it was in hiding. Among ourselves we could argue for hours over who had the best vanilla fudge; but with others, ours was a solid front, and we worked hard to convert those who could look on ice cream as "all the same." Like wine nuts and their vineyard towns in Burgundy, we had our dairy towns to dote on and dally in, and would send others to places like Westminster, Maryland, where even gas stations sell homemade ice cream. We knew that if we were ever in Philadelphia we would head straight for Bassett's in the Reading Terminal. It was Petersen's in Chicago, Gifford's and Avignone Frères in Washington, Bailey's in Boston, the Chocolate Shop in Kalamazoo, and Wil Wright's in Los Angeles. Besides memorizing

Good Humor Corporation
The Good Humor man has performed many duties in his day, but one of the
more unusual is a "pit stop" at a Long Island airfield to fortify a cross-country
racer with ice cream.

names, we developed an ability to sniff out new finds. For instance, it was axiomatic that most universities with dairy schools have a good ice cream shop on the premises. Ours was a cult with leaders, such as Jane Howard who brought us together in her *Life* article, "Confessions of an Ice Cream Eater," in which she spoke for all of us when she said, "I'd drive five hours, and recently did, for a good cone of chocolate chip. I'd make an inconvenient side trip between Kansas City and Chicago, and recently did, for a dish of maple pecan." Her confession was ours, and when she said, "I am an unregenerate ice cream fetishist," we applauded from each nook and cranny of the nation.

In the final analysis, however, it mattered little whether a dip in the economy or some unconscious mammalian lactic urge was behind it all. To the ice-creamaniac what did matter was the lip-smacking reality of the movement to good ice cream spreading across the nation with the firm determination of a glacier. A new ice cream age had begun.

THE ENDLESS SUMMER OF '72, '73, '74 . . .

For the serious ice cream consumer, 1971 was bright and news of coming attractions even brighter. Swensen's of San Francisco announced its plans to go national with its ice cream which it justifiably bills as "outrageously rich." Baskin-Robbins was going international by opening a new front in Canada. Farrell's Toledo-based chain of ice cream parlors was forging new links, as was Atlanta's Dipper Dan, Chicago's Bresler's and other once-local oases of quality. Good Humor opened its first parlor, which it considered a test for a chain of parlors, and the seminally significant Barricini bought up the Loft's candy stores and was installing dipping stands in them. A & P and other supermarkets were experimenting with adding quality ice creams to freezer cabinets that had traditionally held a substance closer to chilled shaving cream than ice cream.

The nation will probably reach a saturation point at some time and the number of new ventures will slow, but when this happens (if it does), Americans should have some remarkable ice creams available in hundreds of flavors. Secure in the knowledge that ice cream has a promising future, it is right and proper that we move on to an account and an appreciation of its rich but seldom-told history. We will take it cone-style, from the top.

II

Up from the Ice Age

I T I S typical of man that he collectively records and remembers far more about his detractors and destroyers than about those who innovate in his behalf. Thus we can put our hands on all sorts of information on plundering armies, rampaging hordes, and lunatic despots, but we have no idea who cranked the first pint of ice cream. About all that we can estimate is that this remarkable person or persons appeared somewhere in Europe—probably in Italy, maybe in England—in the fifteenth or sixteenth century. We do know, however, that ice cream did not originate in the United States as so many unthinking geocentrics have long assumed. Like apple pie (brought from England along with apple seedlings) and certain other edible symbols of America, ice cream had an alien genesis although it was popularized in the United States.

OLD WORLD EVOLUTION

Although the exact origins of ice cream have been lost, enough is known to conclude that its early history was an evolutionary one: first developing from the process of chilling juices and wines, then to primitive water ices and, finally, to chilling concoctions containing milk and cream. Chilled drinks date back many centuries. The Greeks, Romans, and Jews of Palestine were familiar with wine cooled with snow and ice, and we find that Solomon (Proverbs 25:13) liked cool drinks during the warm harvest season. Records indicate that Alexander the Great, during the siege of Petra, had thirty trenches filled with snow and covered with branches so that his ladies would have cool refreshment. This early trend, however, went against the conventional wisdom of the day, which held that there was danger in chilling the body. For example, Hippocrates cautioned:

It is dangerous to heat, cool, or make a commotion all of a sudden in the body, let it be done which way it may, because everything that is excessive is an enemy to nature. Why should anyone run the hazard in the heat of the summer of drinking iced waters which are excessively cold, and suddenly throwing the body into a different state than it was before, producing thereby many ill effects? But, for all this, people will not take warning and most men would rather run the hazard of their lives or health than be deprived of the pleasure of drinking out of ice.

15

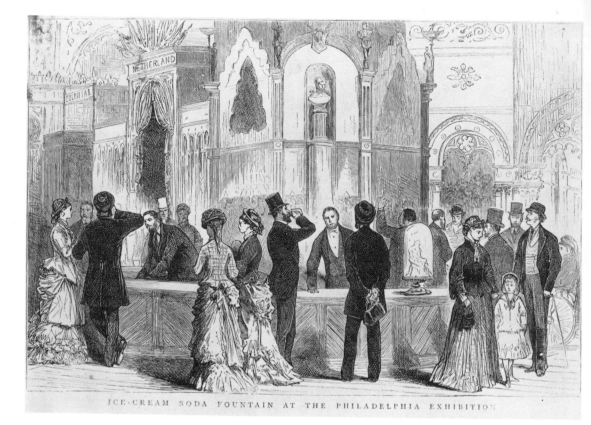

ICE-CREAM SODA FOUNTAIN AT THE PHILADELPHIA EXHIBITION

This wood engraving from the *Graphic* magazine of 1876 celebrates the popularity of James W. Tufts' soda fountain at the Philadelphia Centennial. Tufts paid the then enormous sum of $50,000 to operate his fountain at the exposition.

The first known use of a substance even vaguely resembling ice cream occurred during the rule of Nero Claudius Caesar (A.D. 54–68). Nero periodically sent teams of runners into the mountains for snow, which was relayed back to his table where it was flavored with honey, juices, and fruit pulps. Although this is all that is known, the emperor's dessert was obviously the forerunner of the modern fruit ice. Roman writings of the second century after Christ mention, but never describe, a dish called *mecla*—and it has perplexed scholars ever since the Renaissance. Several have advanced the thesis that it was a frozen or chilled milk concoction.

For the next thousand years there is no recorded mention of anything even suggesting ice cream. Then, at the end of the thirteenth century, Marco Polo returned from the Far East with a recipe for a frozen dessert which included milk and, as far as we can tell today, resembled modern sherbet. The popularity of ices and sherbets grew in Italy and probably evolved into ice cream sometime in the sixteenth century. One description of Italian foods written in 1560 refers to a "food from milk which is made of milk sweetened with honey and frozen. . . . Some persons call it the flower of milk, some call it cream. . . ." If flower of milk was not ice cream it was certainly something close to it.

Frozen desserts are believed to have been brought to France in 1533 by Catherine de Médicis and her retinue when she left Italy at the age of fourteen to marry the Duke of Orléans, who later became Henri II. Through the cooks and chefs she brought with her, she introduced ices and sherbets and possibly ice cream itself to France.

Ice cream reached England at an early date, and just possibly may have predated its appearance in Italy. A manuscript describing the coronation of Henry V mentions a third-course delicacy in the coronation banquet called "crème frez," which at least sounds as though it could be ice cream. If not, ice cream was certainly in Britain in the early seventeenth century when "creme ice" appeared regularly at the table of Charles I. An oft-told, but perhaps apocryphal, story says that Charles was so pleased upon first tasting the dish that he gave the French chef who introduced him to it a pension of twenty pounds sterling a year on the condition that the formula for it be kept secret. The story goes on to say that after Charles was beheaded in 1649, the chef sold the secret to a consortium of noblemen who had long coveted it. James II, Charles's son, apparently shared his father's passion, as the accounts of the Lord Steward's department for 1686 show an entry for "a dozen dishes of ice cream" which were purchased for James while he was camped at Hounslow Heath and priced at an unconscionable one pound per dish.

The first substantial piece of writing on ice cream was an anonymous 84-page manuscript entitled *L'Art de Faire des Glaces* which, through watermarks in the paper, has been dated "circa 1700." It is a "how to" work of some sophistication, giving detailed instructions for the preparation of such delights as apricot, violet, rose, chocolate, and caramel ice creams and water ices. A number of British cookbooks of the eighteenth century contain ice cream formulas. One such work is Mrs. Hanna Glasse's *The Art of Cookery Made Easy* (1747)—considered by scholars to be the first major cookbook written by a woman in what was until then an almost exclusively male domain.* In 1768

---

* Mrs. Glasse's formula well illustrates the practices of the period. Her recipe: "Take two Pewter Basons, one larger than the other; the inward one must have a

there appeared in Paris what is undoubtedly the most outlandish treatise on the subject ever to be published. Called *The Art of Making Frozen Desserts,* it is a 240-page offering by one M. Emy, who not only gives formulas for "food fit for the gods," but offers theological and philosophical explanations for such phenomena as the freezing of water. The tone of the book is set by its frontispiece, which depicts a brace of angels delivering ice cream to earth from heaven.

Although frozen desserts were becoming common in regal circles, not until 1670 when the Café Procope opened in Paris did "iced creams" and sherbets spread to the masses. Founded by a Sicilian, Francesco Procopio dei Coltelli (Procope for short), the café not only introduced the new type of dessert but was credited with being that city's first coffeehouse, or café. Coltelli had opened his trend-setting establishment after a long career as a Paris *limonadier*. At the time he was one of 250 master *limonadiers* who were organized as a trade guild, suggesting that perhaps the city was glutted with lemonade and that he shrewdly opted for something novel with a more promising future. Café Procope is still in operation today on the rue de l'Ancienne Comédie, as is the Caffè Florian on the Piazza San Marco in Venice, among the first of the Italian coffeehouses and reputedly Coltelli's source of inspiration. During the next hundred years a succession of new cafés appeared in Paris, many of which had their own house ice cream specialty. From the Café Napolitain on the Boulevard des Italiens came the macaroon, rum, and ice

---

close Cover, into which you are to put your Cream, and mix it with Raspberries or whatever you like best, to give it a Flavour and a Colour. Sweeten it to your Palate; then cover it close, and set it into the larger Bason. Fill it with Ice and a Handful of Salt; let it stand in this Ice three Quarters of an Hour, then uncover it, and stir the Cream well together; cover it close again and let it stand Half an Hour longer, after that turn it to your Plate. These things are made at the Pewterers."

cream concoction named for its proprietor, an Italian named Tortoni.

During the eighteenth century ice cream began appearing in other parts of Europe. From Vienna, for example, Lady Mary Wortley Montagu wrote in 1716 of "ice cream in several forms, both winter and summer." And from the same city, Beethoven observed in a note in 1794: "It is very warm here. The Viennese are afraid that it will soon be impossible to have any ice cream, for as winter is mild, ice is rare."

ICE CREAM COMES TO THE NEW WORLD

The first appearance of ice cream in America is not known, but the first record of any sort indicating its presence in the colonies is a letter, written in 1700 by a guest of Governor William Bladen of Maryland, which states: ". . . we had dessert no less Curious; among the Rarities of which it was Compos'd was some fine Ice Cream which, with the Strawberries and Milk, eat most Deliciously."

So far as is known, the first public advertisement of ice cream anywhere in the world was paid for by Philip Lenzi, a confectioner, who announced in the New York *Gazette* of May 12, 1777, that his ice cream "may be had almost every day." It can be assumed that ice cream was gaining a toehold in New York during the 1780s, because other ads began appearing in the New York papers. In 1781, a Lenzi competitor named Joseph Corre was the first to advertise the words ICE CREAM in large conspicuous letters, and an announcement in the New York *Post Boy* (1786) read: "Ladies and Gentlemen may be supplied with ice

The Bettmann Archive

Bowery urchins of the last century partake from a street vendor or hokey-pokey man. Attesting to the popularity of ice cream among poorer Americans, a 1901 newspaper article said, ''Thriftless, but affectionate, is the lower class parent. Shoes the child must do without. . . . But here is five cents to buy hokey-pokey. That much he can afford.''

cream every day at the City Tavern by their humble servant Joseph Crowe." Commenting on the significance of these early ads, two American dairy historians, H. A. Schuette and Francis J. Robinson of the Laboratory of Foods and Sanitation at the University of Wisconsin, wrote in 1933: "But quite apart from the antiquarian interest which attaches to these advertisements is the fact that they were in a sense prophetic of the day when the adopted home of ice cream was to outstrip the countries of its origin in the degree to which it was to be developed and in the popularity accorded it by Americans. . . ."

Within a few years, the French gourmet Anthelme Brillat-Savarin returned from a trip to New York to report that the ice cream ladle was helping to create an American *nouveau riche*. In his classic *La Physiologie du Goût*, he devotes a chapter to French nobility in exile who made their living from food, and wrote: "Capitaine Collet made a great deal of money in New York, during the years 1794 and 1795, by selling ice cream and sherbet to the inhabitants of that busy city. The ladies especially never tired of a pleasure so novel to them; nothing was more amusing than to watch them smirk and simper as they tasted it. They could not understand how it could be kept so cold. . . ."

Considerable evidence has come to light indicating that George Washington possessed more than a passing fancy for ice cream. It is known that he was served ice cream by Mrs. Alexander Hamilton at a dinner party in 1789 and that the inventory at his home at Mount Vernon contained "two pewter ice cream pots." The fact has also been unearthed that when he was in Philadelphia attending a meeting of the Society of the Cincinnati, he bought something called a "Cream Machine for

The International Association of Ice Cream Manufacturers
An early delivery van from the Hendler Creamery Co. The Hendler family
was responsible for supplying generations of Baltimorians with ice cream,
and the late L. Manuel Hendler was chairman of the Ice Cream Centennial
celebrations in 1951.

Making Ice''—which sounds as though it might have been some sort of an ice cream–producing device. Most impressive of all, however, are the records of an ice cream merchant on Chatham Street in New York, which show that Washington ran up a tab of £51/6s./2d.—about $200—for ice cream during the summer of 1790. Similarly, Thomas Jefferson has left evidence of a proclivity for ice cream, which includes his own eighteen-step recipe for ice cream and a favored way of having it served, namely, to enclose it in cases of warm pastry.

While ice cream had graced the tables of presidents before, it was Dolley Madison who glamorized it by first serving it at the White House at state dinners.* An impressionable guest describes it with convincing effect: ''Last night I was bid by our President to the White House, and it was a most unusual affair. Mrs. Madison always entertains with Grace and Charm, but last night there was a sparkle in her eye that set astir an Air of Expectancy among her Guests. When finally the brilliant Assemblage—America's best—entered the dining room, they beheld a Table set with French china and English silver, laden with good things to eat, and in the Centre high on a silver platter, a large, shining dome of pink Ice Cream.''

For many years ice cream was a dish of the very wealthy in America, an eighteenth-century rarity and delicacy of the highest order. Not only was ice difficult to come by during most of the year; even with an ample supply of ice, ice cream was ever so difficult to make. Commonly it was made by the ''pot freezer'' method, an especially awkward process in which the mixture was

---

* A black cook named Augustus Jackson, who learned to make ice cream at the White House, later became one of the ice cream pioneers of Philadelphia when, in 1832, he started one of the first retail ice cream shops in the city.

vigorously beaten in a pot at the same time that the pot was shaken up and down in a large pan of salt and ice. Two early nineteenth-century developments changed the situation.

First, "ice harvesting" and the insulated icehouse became widespread, and that precious commodity became much more common. The number of confectioners who sold ice cream increased and ice cream parlors began appearing in major cities. For instance, the April 20, 1808, issue of the *Louisiana Courier* (New Orleans) carried the notice: "Ice creams may be had at the Coffee-House every day between the hours of 12 and 9 o'clock." That the famous Exchange Coffee-House at Chatres and St. Louis streets was the first recorded Southern establishment offering the delicacy was brought about by the fact that ice was beginning to be harvested in the winter along the Ohio River and taken to New Orleans, where it was stored in insulated icehouses for summertime consumption. Besides the ice cream parlor, the advent of this new ice-rich age also brought with it another venerable ice cream institution, the street vendor. In the summer of 1828 the *National Advertiser* pointed out that a group of boisterous fellows with kettles in their hands had added, "I Scream, Ice Cream" to the varied collection of New York City street cries.

Second, in 1846 Nancy Johnson, an innovative woman about whom we know little, invented the hand-cranked ice cream freezer, which was essentially a cumbersome version of the same home ice cream freezers that sell in large quantities to this day. Although the task of cranking ice cream was an arduous one, making it that way in a bucket was a vast improvement over earlier methods. However, for reasons that have never been made clear, Nancy Johnson did not patent her invention, and on

Buying a Peerless Freezer

WITH THE

Vacuum Screw Dasher.

Write us for information; it costs nothing and may save you money.

Our recently published booklet " **Fifty Ices,**" gives full description of the Peerless, with illustrations and price list.

PEERLESS FREEZER CO., Cincinnati, O.

CLAD'S ICE CREAM DISHERS.

Fig. No. E 6559.

With Seamless Stamped Bowl.

May 30, 1848, William G. Young registered it with the Patent Office. Young at least had the courtesy to call his product the "Johnson Patent Ice-Cream Freezer."

The familiar "Johnson-Young" crank-and-paddle freezer in a bucket was an immediate sensation, bringing ice cream making into the realm of the average citizen. Commenting on the mixer in 1850, the editor of the then-popular magazine *Godey's Lady's Book* announced that ice cream had become one of the necessities of life. "A party without it would be like a breakfast without bread or a dinner without a roast." The popularity of the device was such that Young was given a run for his money. Within a few years, there were many imitations and "improved" versions on the market, and dozens of other patents had been issued on hand-cranked freezers. An 1851 Philadelphia cookbook gave added credence to the fact that ice cream was coming into its own, as it contained recipes for no less than thirty-four different ice creams and eighteen different water ices, while earlier cookbooks seldom contained more than one or two, if any, such formulas.

Ice cream had become popular in the United States by mid-century—so much so that Ralph Waldo Emerson was prompted to write of the national character, "We dare not trust our wit for making our house pleasant to our friend so we buy ice cream." The stage was set for the birth of a full-fledged ice cream industry.

III

The Annals of American
Ice Cream (1851-1941)

ODAY THE American ice cream industry is a mammoth entity annually producing more than enough ice cream to fill the Grand Canyon. Each American man, woman, and child consumes a yearly average of twenty-three quarts of ice cream, ice milk, sherbet, ices, and other commercially produced frozen dairy products. Except for Australians, Canadians, and New Zealanders, no other people eat nearly half that much. In fact, if the average annual intake of two Frenchmen, two Austrians, an Italian, a Belgian, and a Briton were added together, the total would still be two pints and a few Good Humors short of the American average. This giant American industry got off to a humble start over one hundred years ago when the average American tongue could expect to taste less than a teaspoon of it a year.

SUCCESS À LA MODE

The ice cream industry began as a problem of supply and demand was solved. A moderately successful Baltimore milk dealer named Jacob Fussell had long been finding himself over-supplied with cream. The problem stemmed from the fact that his dairies were giving him a constant supply of it whereas its pattern of sales was highly erratic. By 1851 the problem was such that it threatened Fussell's business and he was hard pressed for a solution. After exploring several possibilities, he decided that his surplus could be profitably disposed of as ice cream for 25 cents a quart, which compared dramatically with the prevailing price of 65 cents a quart charged by the city caterers and others who made and sold ice cream in very small quantities.

In short order, Fussell found that his ice cream business was more profitable than milk, and he lost no time in converting his entire plant to the production of ice cream, thus making him the first full-fledged manufacturer/wholesaler in the field. By 1856 he had prospered to the point where he set up another plant in Washington; within a few years he opened one in Boston and, finally, founded the first wholesale ice cream operation in New York. While Fussell inaugurated the ice cream industry in the East, he also had a direct impact on the westward movement of the industry. Perry Brazelton, a banker and close friend who had fallen on hard times after the Panic of 1857, was taken in by Fussell and tutored in the business. Like a latter-day Johnny Appleseed, Brazelton successfully moved the industry to Cincinnati, Chicago, and St. Louis.

A fashionable ice cream parlor of the late nineteenth century, by which time people of all ages and financial situations indulged in what was becoming the national dessert.

The father of the American ice cream industry was a man of strong conviction. He was a fiery force in the Abolition movement, working actively in the underground railway. His public antislavery speeches were such that after one of them he narrowly escaped a Baltimore mob that charged into his office to lynch him. A close friend of Abraham Lincoln, he was a delegate to the Republican convention that nominated him. A frugal, dour-faced Quaker who peppered his writings with thee's and thou's, he gave much of his fortune to charity; for instance, he built and paid for Fussell Court, a housing project for newly freed slaves. He was, however, an uncompromising capitalist who, for example, attempted to fix the retail price of a quart of ice cream in New York at an uncharitable $1.25, threatening to annihilate any confectioner who did not comply. The confectioners rebelled *en masse* and Fussell's plot was foiled.

THE UNCRANKING OF A GIANT

Despite the early success enjoyed by Fussell, Brazelton, and others, the industry grew very slowly and many populous states did not have their first ice cream company until 1880 or later. Ice cream fanciers in such states as Delaware, Arkansas, and Montana did not see their first factory-made ice cream until the early 1900s. The reason for this sluggishness was that as late as the 1880s the ice cream plant was little more than a very large hand-cranked freezer. F. D. Hutchinson, who opened Iowa's first ice cream plant, recalled some years later: "I remember that on the Fourth of July in 1890 we shipped out three hundred gallons of ice cream—all frozen by hand."

Young lady buying frozen dainties from a hokey-pokey man about 1910. *The Dictionary of American Slang* defines ''hokey-pokey'' as ''Cheap ice cream, candy, confections, primarily made to be attractive to children.''

Not until the turn of the century did the industry begin to grow dramatically, which it did for about a decade, when the pace accelerated from dramatic to phenomenal. A five-million-gallon-a-year babe in 1899, industry production shot up to thirty million gallons in 1909 and topped 150 million gallons in 1919. This remarkable growth was occasioned by a quick, steady procession of technical developments which transformed the ice cream plant to a practical profit-promising operation. One after another, mechanical and technical revolutions occurred. First came practical steam power, then mechanical refrigeration, the homogenizer, electric power and electric motors, sophisticated test equipment, packaging machines, new freezers and freezing processes, new insulation concepts, and the motorized delivery van. The net result of all of this was that by the early 1920s the ice cream plant was nearly as modernized as the ones that exist today.

Along with growth and technical change came a group of ancillary institutions to support the burgeoning industry. *The Ice Cream Review* and *The Ice Cream Trade Journal* were founded to give the industry its news. Courses in ice cream making became common in agricultural schools. Most important, state, regional, and national trade associations were started to boost and promote ice cream and fight the ambitious regulations being proposed by state governments and the U.S. Department of Agriculture. As an industry it defeated the institution of federal standards, attempts to have ice cream sold by weight (rather than volume), and ingredient labeling.

By the 1920s ice cream was fast becoming what industry leaders liked to call it, "America's typical food." It was dispensed everywhere from the corner drugstore soda fountain to the Pullman car. The ice cream soda, sundae, and banana split

33

seemed to grow more popular each day and the particularly American craft of the soda jerk was coming into its own as an indigenous folk art. Everyone was eating ice cream, and noteworthy Americans extolled its virtues. In the world of sports, for example, the incomparable Walter Johnson boasted that all he ate on the day he was to pitch was a quart of ice cream. Others —among them Babe Ruth, Ty Cobb, and Pablo Nurmi, "the Flying Finn"—gave unsolicited testimonials to their favorite dish. In keeping with the prohibitionist litany of the era, a popular story asserted that when the fast, lithe, ice cream–stoked "Gentleman Jim" Corbett defeated the great, booze-loving John L. Sullivan, the latter reformed and ate ice cream until his dying day. The Corbett/Sullivan tale was one of many parables of the era in which a healthy dairy product emerged to KO John Barleycorn. Such stories helped ice cream, but they were nothing compared to the windfall of Prohibition itself.

That the nation was opting for ice cream instead of beer and liquor was looked upon in the industry as a heartwarming development. Not only were the pooh-bahs of ice cream pleased with the promise of new profits, there was the added dividend of smug self-righteousness associated with weaning the nation away from the hard stuff onto the cold stuff.* During the early days of Prohibition the trade journals regularly compiled lists of breweries that had been turned into ice cream plants, and the leaders of the industry proclaimed their zealous satisfaction in verse and prose. Indicative of the mood was a song first introduced at the Pacific Ice Cream Manufacturers Convention in

---

* There were, of course, wayward ice cream parlormen who saw their establishments as the perfect cover for liquor sales. In Philadelphia, long a center of ice cream innovation, a series of federal raids closed parlors specializing in ice cream sodas with a kick.

Portland in November, 1920, which became a convention standard during the Volstead era and was sung to the tune of "Old Black Joe." It went like this:

> Gone are the days when Father was a souse,
> Gone are the days of the weekly family rows,
> Gone from this land since prohibition's here—
> He brings a brick of ice cream home instead of beer.
> CHORUS
> He's coming, he's coming; we can see him coming near—
> He brings a brick of ice cream home instead of beer.

The 1920s, an era of prosperity and frivolity, saw ice cream expanding into new territory and gaining new popularity. Indicative was the 1921 decision by the Commissioner of Ellis Island to treat all immigrants to a taste of something truly American upon arriving in the land of promise: as part of their first meal in America they were served ice cream. Reporting on a meal for 1,700 new arrivals, *The Ice Cream Review* said that many were tenderly spreading this sweet, cool "new butter" on their bread with knives. Ice cream was moving into every nook and cranny of the land. For instance, in the Missouri and Arkansas Ozarks it had long been a delicacy and the ice cream social a major event. Ice cream was a rare commodity there, since its production was completely dependent on the vicissitudes of weather. Thus the winter social could be held only after harsh periods when mountain streams had frozen, and in the summer it had to be hastily arranged after hailstorms covered the land with enough large, hard pellets to be collected and used. Traditionally, Ozark ice cream had been made by agitating tin sorghum buckets placed in boxes filled with salted ice. This all changed in the 1920s as the ice cream truck began nosing its way into the hills.

In addition others of missionary zeal found new markets for American ice cream overseas. One such citizen, Paul S. Crawley, introduced ice cream to China by way of his shop in Shanghai, and during his first year in operation sold nine thousand gallons of ice cream and over a million Eskimo Pies. Complete soda fountains—replete with Tennessee-marble counters and banks of syrup pumps—were exported in volume to nations as far away as Japan and Chile. Ice cream mixes and equipment were bringing the cool dish to South America, and American technicians went to Europe, the cradle of the frozen dessert, to help bring production techniques out of the nineteenth century.

By 1929 Americans were downing an unprecedented nine quarts apiece per year and ice cream had steadily grown as a vital commercial force in its own right. The small plant, the street vendor (or hokey-pokey man, as he was called in many cities), and the dairyman selling homemade ice cream from his barn on weekends were giving way to large dairy combines and corporations listed on the New York Stock Exchange.

So important was the product and the shifting fancies of the American ice cream consumer that economies of smaller nations were virtually dominated by the American soda fountain and ice cream parlor. Vanilla became a hot item of international commerce, and there was rejoicing in several republics as the banana split became the thing an American bought when he wanted to splurge after the movies. This *de facto* ice cream imperialism reached such a stage in the late 1920s that the U.S. Department of Commerce was able to report that the fantastic popularity of the Eskimo Pie and other chocolate-jacketed novelties lifted the

Eskimo Pie Corp.
Tin Pan Alley responded to the popularity of ice cream with songs like this and the immortal "I Scream, You Scream, We All Scream for Ice Cream."

cocoa-dependent economy of Ecuador out of depression into a period of recovery. But Ecuador's respite was short-lived, for as America awoke to the Great Depression, the nickels and dimes needed for ice cream became harder and harder to shake loose.

THE BUBBLE MELTS

Not only did the depression itself have an adverse effect on the ice cream industry, but on its heels came a series of events and conditions that compounded the problem, with the net result that by 1933 the per-capita production had dropped to almost half its 1929 level. Frozen custard, or "frozen fluff" as it was then called, emerged as one major "new menace" to ice cream sales. The advent of home refrigeration in the late 1920s and early 1930s brought with it a vogue for homemade ice cream and ices while at the same time new equipment—such as the counter ice cream freezer—saw a new group of retail ice creamers who offered the product homemade on the premises.

In 1933 the Twenty-first Amendment, repealing Prohibition, was ratified, thus setting off considerable panic in the industry, which believed that ice cream would be the major casualty in an impending national binge. Industry leaders cautioned against despair and sought out ways to rebound when beer and liquor hit the streets. In a typical pep-talk of the period the industry was asked by the editors of *The Ice Cream Review,* "Are we going to sit around and cry on each other's shoulders and assure each other that the industry will now surely go to the bow-wows?" The editors answered with a resounding No! and called for creative thinking, even going so far as to suggest new strategies ranging from billing ice cream as a "morning after" remedy to the creation of unlikely mergers in drinks containing liquor and ice cream or sherbet. Best-forgotten concoctions like "Iced Tea Tango," "The Bêrmuda Sling," and "Cherry Nectar" were unveiled to ensure ice cream's part in the upcoming booze bath. Obnoxious combinations like "Comin' Through the Rye" * did not become national fads; fortunately, as the nation became "wet" again, the industry did not falter and fold. To be sure, repeal was a strong blow and sales were affected, as *The Ice Cream Review* reported sadly in late 1934: "The dime that went for soda now frequently goes for beer."

Still another problem that faced the industry was the ice cream bootlegger, who came into prominence as the beer bootlegger faded into history. This new figure was described in a 1933 issue of *Business Week:* "He's usually a small, often a hole-in-the-wall manufacturer who makes ice cream after his own standards—which may or may not be those prescribed by state laws—and sells it to dealers for less than the popular advertised brands cost them." In many cases bootleggers were able to persuade dealers to substitute their often hideous ice cream for the product of the bona-fide manufacturer. The problem never really got out of control, since the bootleggers were constantly running afoul of local laws and standards requirements. In New York City

---

* For the curious and courageous here is the long-forgotten formula for "Comin' Through the Rye." It is printed here rather than in the formulary that appears later in the book because it does not merit being put in the same gallery with such fountain masterpieces as the "Broadway" and the "Banana Skyscraper."

> 1 ounce rye
> 1 serving vanilla ice cream
> Ginger ale

Place first two ingredients in tall glass. Fill with ginger ale. Stir quickly. Serve at once.

alone during March and April of 1933, 899 bootleggers were con-
victed. Nevertheless, before the situation was cleared up, some
mighty nasty ice cream had crossed the national palate.

But despite booze, bootleggers, and bad times, the industry
was showing signs of recovery. By 1935 hardsell and enthusiastic
boosterism were registering increases in per-capita consumption, with the result that the industry emerged early from the
depression; while 1935 was not another 1928 saleswise, 1937 was.

Of all the ice cream boosting in the 1930s none could compare with what was coming out of Hollywood. Fred Astaire and
Ginger Rogers tied up with Borden's to promote the "Hollywood
Lunch"—the noontime repast of a sandwich and a malted—and
thirty thousand soda fountains carried huge cutouts of the popular couple promoting their favorite lunch together with the film
The Gay Divorcée. Then there was the giant boost accorded by
Kid Millions starring Eddie Cantor, which came out in 1934 and
treated an estimated twenty million moviegoers to an all-color,
talking picture with an extended ice cream fantasy for its finale.
The scene takes place in a most extraordinary ice cream factory
where a chorus of beautiful girls carries chocolate, vanilla, and
strawberries to a mammoth freezer as another troop of scantily
clad lovelies skates across the freezer top and still others coast
about on huge slabs of Neapolitan ice cream. Stage center is a
young, philanthropic Cantor treating hundreds of waifs to an
opulent ice cream banquet while a reformed gangster shoots
cherries onto each youngster's helping from a machine gun.
"Kid Millions" sodas and sundaes were a big item nationally
and then-mayor Jackson of Baltimore was so carried away by the
film that he declared a special "Ice Cream Week" in his city.

Right through the 1940s ice cream and celluloid proved to

Library of Congress
Good Humor man serving customers in Washington, D.C., in 1942. With new trucks not available and parts hard to get during World War II, Good Humor nonetheless kept rolling throughout the war.

be an inspired match. On the screen the small-town soda fountain became an important setting for action in family-oriented films of the Andy Hardy genre, and the real life soda fountain was the place to go after the movie. The fountain at Schwab's Drugstore at Hollywood and Vine was Hollywood incarnate, and it was to this shrine that ambitious beauties from Middle America came to be discovered. Schwab's was written into so many scripts as a set that Paramount had the fountain reproduced on its own backlot. Even staid ice cream industry publications went Hollywood and stopped carrying pictures of Vogt Continuous Process Freezers and Mojonnier Overrun Testers on their covers. *The Ice Cream Review* was able to boast one string of four covers which went from Madeleine Carroll to Bette Davis, Claudette Colbert, and finally Dorothy Lamour—each eating ice cream. For reasons obscured by time, Paramount and Columbia publicists specialized in turning out 8 x 10 glossies of starlets licking cones (perhaps some mogul's idea of the perfect blend of the girl-next-door and cool sensuality).

Other breaks for ice cream just happened or were made to happen by industry leaders and innovators. President Franklin D. Roosevelt publicly confessed in 1935 that he liked to have ice cream at least once a day. Infant airlines like Pan Am, Eastern, and TWA began booking ice cream on their flights. Sales gimmicks galore appeared, ranging from the Ice Cream Telegram— a molded ice cream replica of a Western Union telegram delivered to the home—to sundaes with hot toppings to sell in the slack winter months. National dairy and ice cream associations traded on the healthy nature of ice cream, pushing it as an item high in nutrition and low in cost.

The International Association of Ice Cream Manufacturers,

the industry's prime trade association, and the Ice Cream Merchandising Institute, the Association's merchandising affiliate, teamed up to put a new polish on the soda fountain. Regional seminars, called Sundae Schools, were held to introduce the latest in new fountain concoctions and sales-generating ideas. These new ideas came out of the Institute's Washington laboratory (best described as the ultimate soda fountain) where such edibles as the "Four Tower Sundae" and "Dad's Day Sundae" were researched and developed along with such hardware as a specially designed banana split bowl. Such was the attention to detail and perfection at the lab that well-rendered diagrams were sent out along with the formulas for new concoctions. Behind this remarkable operation, which continued at full tilt after World War II, was George W. Hennerich, whom *Business Week* termed the "Human Dynamo of the Ice Cream Industry."

The effect of much of this promotion did not translate into sales because the nation went on war rationing and shortages sharply limited the supply. However, this did not mean that the nation was not thinking about ice cream.

IV

Ice Cream and the Modern Era (1941-1971)

As early as 1789 the American soldier looked upon ice cream as something special. Historian Harry Emerson Wildes wrote that, after victory at the Battle of Fallen Timbers, Major General "Mad" Anthony Wayne and his officers sat down to a feast that ended with "dishes of ice cream, a dainty which the Army had not seen since it left the East."

Later, during the Civil War, none other than Jacob Fussell was selling ice cream to Union supply officers from his Washington plant. It was during World War I that ice cream first got official army endorsement as a "morale food," and no less a person than the Secretary of War made periodic announcements as to the availability of ice cream for American troops. So popular was ice cream that firms were founded near large domestic bases just to supply them, and the situation was such in late 1917 that the military was buying so much ice cream that it became a matter for "competitive bidding," thereby elevating it to the status of an important wartime matériel. On the home front, ice cream was officially decreed an "essential foodstuff" by the government and none of its components were rationed within the industry.

Much later, during the 1950s, the Pentagon was prompted to come out foursquare on the side of ice cream as food for its fighting men. The policy question was raised by the late General Lewis B. "Chesty" Puller, who led the First Marine Regiment in the early months of the Korean War, when in a Patton-like gesture he announced that his marines "don't get ice cream." Puller stated that the nation's troops were being pampered and suggested "beer and whiskey" as the proper fuel for what he disdainfully termed "the ice cream and candy Marines." Organizations ranging from the Women's Christian Temperance Union to veterans' groups howled at Puller's intemperate remarks, with the general feeling being summed up by a VFW commander, who was quoted in the New York *Times* as saying, "Puller is 100 percent wrong. Ice cream doesn't make a man a sissy. It's in the American tradition." In April, 1952, shortly after the original statement, the Pentagon moved to close the debate by announcing a scheme by which ice cream would appear in Korean mess lines at least three times a week.*

By the time of the war in Vietnam, military ice cream production had developed to a level of sophistication that began to

---

* Undeterred, Puller continued the litany after returning to the States and, besides continued snorting about the "ice cream Marines," was widely reported in the press to have gone around Camp Pendleton smashing candy machines.

seem more like a McNamara weapons system than a dessert production. Included in the ice cream arsenal was everything from a big Foremost Dairy plant near Saigon to a compact little freezer, built to military specifications for use in remote areas, that could crank out 2.5 gallons of ice cream in ten minutes. Ice cream had become such an element of military planning that a scheme to install thirty small ice cream plants in the Pleiku area by 1968 was given the martial code name of "Operation Deep Freeze."

Despite all this attention to ice cream during other periods of national stress and mobilization, none can compare with World War II, when ice cream was at once an edible symbol for good morale, for what was being fought for, and for America itself. It represented home and all that was wholesome and happy, and for that reason was what GI's wrote home about, what their pin-ups lapped from cones, and what the boy-heroes of the era's motion pictures dreamed about in their innocent dreams.

SYMBOL IN A SCOOP

During World War II the symbol of ice cream was flashed home in all shapes, sizes, and tones as the press carried a steady diet of ice cream stories. The nation was told that for every pilot rescued from the water by an escort destroyer, aircraft carriers would give the smaller ship a twenty-gallon reward. Newspaper after newspaper carried quotes from hometown boys, like this one from the Altoona, Pennsylvania, *Tribune:*

The first thing I'm going to do when I get back in the good old USA is to find the prettiest girl in town and

sit myself down to a mess of hamburgers with everything on them, and divide my time looking at her and
wolfing down hamburgers with dishes of ice cream on
the side.

And from the narrator in *Thirty Seconds over Tokyo,* when it
first appeared in *Collier's,* we learned:

One of the things I often thought about during the tough
days . . . was ice cream and apple pie. Kid stuff, but
it preyed on my mind so much that I swore that if I got
out to a big city I'd eat myself glassy-eyed on apple
pie à la mode.

From time to time ice cream even became headline material:
"SOLDIER DREAMS OF WHOLE MOUNTAINS OF ICE CREAM," *bannered*
the Memphis *Press Scimitar.* "SOUTH PACIFIC WOUNDED WANT
ICE CREAM FIRST," said the St. Louis *Globe-Democrat.* And from
the Pittsburgh *Press* came "THEIR IDEA OF HEAVEN"—an allu-
sion to what airmen define as "a place where ice cream abounds
and flak and fighters are forgotten." Headlines even got headline
treatment: "BIGGER NEWS THAN THE WAR" was the head of an
AP story of 1944 which reported on a *Stars and Stripes* banner,
"ICE CREAM SODAS SOON IN EUROPEAN THEATRE OF OPERATION."
The Boston *Globe* covered the same development with large letters reading, "ARMY WILL SEND 'BLACK COWS' TO YANKS IN
ENGLAND"—going on to report that the army was looking for
American soda jerks of long experience to hire as overseas con-
sultants on such GI dreams as the "Black Cow" and the "Broad-
way."

The popularity of ice cream in the wartime navy was such
that in 1945 the navy commissioned the world's first "floating

ice cream parlor'' for service in the western Pacific. Built at a cost of over one million dollars, the parlor was a concrete barge capable of producing ten gallons of ice cream every seven seconds. If the floating parlor was evidence of the navy's official recognition of ice cream as a very special substance, it could not compare with the spontaneous testimonial delivered by the crew of the aircraft carrier *Lexington* when it was mortally damaged and the order was given to abandon ship. Someone remembered that the ship was carrying a large stock of ice cream and suggested that the crew get its licks in before the ship went down. Word spread quickly and the cans of ice cream were hustled up onto the carrier's flight deck. The sailors dug in and many were still eating ice cream as they scrambled down the nets cast over the side of the ship. Navy units outdid themselves in coming up with ingenious means of getting ice cream.* For example, in 1944 a seabee battalion in North Africa put together a gargantuan ice cream machine that provided 168,000 portions before it broke down. It had been built from the cast-off equipment of war: German motor, Italian gears, and U.S. tractor parts.

The navy was not alone in its ice cream bias, for each service seemed to be vying for the title of most determined admirer, most avid consumer, and most ingenious provider of ice cream. Word came via the New York *Times* in 1943 that airmen based in Britain had stumbled upon a novel means of production. These men were placing ice cream mixtures in large cans stowed in the rear gunner's compartments in B-29s where the combination of

* One particular ice cream innovator of the period was a navy PX operator in the New Hebrides who wangled an ice cream freezer from an aircraft-carrier supply officer and then proceeded to use local fruits and flavors for exotic and unheard-of flavor combinations. He was the late Burt Baskin, co-founder of Baskin-Robbins and flavor genius extraordinaire. We will say more about him later.

the plane's vibration and the freezing effect of high-altitude fly-ing yielded an especially smooth and creamy ice cream. Even the Marine Corps got into the act, albeit with one of the more sordid versions of the story. Late in the war, it was dutifully reported in *The Ice Cream Review,* marine commanders in the Pacific found that one of the only ways to stop "souvenir hunting" in combat areas was to offer ice cream as a reward for not doing so.

Not only was ice cream the symbol for all that was good in America, its absence was a symbolic reminder of all that was wrong in the world. As the clouds of war gathered during the summer of 1941, the warlords in Tokyo let it be known that ice cream was to be dispensed with. In true totalitarian style, au-thorities dropped the controlled price of ice cream sodas and sundaes from 20 sen to 13—a move calculated to force vendors out of business, thereby ridding the nation of a needless luxury. On the Allied side, the demands of war had produced shortages of such severity that in 1942 ice cream was banned outright in Britain. In the United States ice cream was still available to civilians, but limited by stringent rules and conditions. The in-dustry cut itself back to twenty flavors to simplify distribution, deliveries were reduced to conserve rationed truck tires, and the government was forced to reduce the milk and sugar available for ice cream. Shortages were common and many a neighborhood soda parlor found itself without ice cream intermittently.

Domestic American ice cream had gone to war for the dura-tion, and that fact could not be missed. Periodicals ranging from the New York *Times* to the women's magazines put editors to work on special ice cream formulas that did not use items in short supply. Within the industry, fountain innovators rallied with elaborate concoctions which relied on those ingredients that were either not rationed or were superabundant; the result was specials like the Honeydew Dip and the Honeymoon Special. From Washington the Ice Cream Merchandising Institute successfully launched a ''Victory Sundaes'' drive with its slogan ''Keep 'Em Buying to Keep 'Em Flying.'' The drive was an admixture of profit and patriotism in which sundaes—preferably the specially designed ''All-American''—were sold, with a 10-cent Defense Savings Stamp attached, for 10 cents above the normal retail price of a sundae.

This era was brought to a close with the symbolic 44-foot-high, 16-foot-wide, 3,500-cubic-foot helium-filled balloon shaped like a triple-decker ice cream cone that appeared in Macy's 1945 Thanksgiving Parade. Billed as the world's largest cone, its image was carried by wirephoto to papers across the nation, signaling the end of a period in which ice cream was adored in the abstract and the beginning of a period of ice cream consumption never equaled before or after.

THE GREAT ICE CREAM ORGY OF 1946

As rationing ended and raw materials became plentiful again, the nation started upon an unprecedented ice cream orgy. In 1946 over twenty quarts of ice cream were produced for each American. This was twice that being produced at the beginning of the war, and though recent years have seen per-capita production for all frozen desserts—ice cream, ice milk, sherbet, etc.— go over twenty quarts, there has never been a year to compare with '46 for consumption of straight ice cream.

The public was not alone in its excesses; the industry had

its own orgy of expectations into which it whipped itself with boosterish behavior calculated to embarrass a Babbitt. Its major rallying point was the "billion gallon year," a crusade which *The Ice Cream Review* talked about in such apostolic terms as these:

> It can be done. It will be done. Let us go up and possess this billion gallon land in less than five years. . . . True, you will profit in dollars and cents by making a success of this crusade, your crusade. But you will get an equal or even greater degree of satisfaction by having the Public enjoy and benefit from the use of more and still more ice cream, "Milk in Its Finest Form."

To support such dreams, grown men sat down for large ice cream breakfasts at industry conventions to serve as an example to the youth of the nation, and industry technicians trafficked in "super ice creams"—ice cream enriched with all nine vitamins needed by man, ice cream laced with minerals then in vogue, and penicillin ice cream. The latter development was touted in the trade press as just one of many medicinal/merchandising possibilities on the rosy postwar horizon.

If 1946 had been a great year for ice cream, 1947 was a very good one, and 1948 was a pretty good year. The postwar passion for ice cream had died down to a relatively steady urge, which has been relatively steady ever since. The orgy was over and the industry was settling into maturity. Significantly, the industry celebrated its centennial in 1951, one hundred years after Jacob Fussell had opted for ice cream over milk.

The biggest of the centennial events took place in June in Baltimore at the exact spot where Fussell's business had first stood. It was a festive affair of the first order. Free ice cream was dished out, and the youngsters of Baltimore mingled with hundreds of industry bigwigs and VIPs who had come to mark the occasion. Piper Laurie and Tony Curtis were crowned "Sweethearts of the Ice Cream Industry," songs were sung, proclamations were read, and Mrs. Carrie Fussell Craft, the 84-year-old daughter of Jacob Fussell, unveiled a bronze tablet in honor of her father, which still stands embedded in concrete at the corner of Hillen and Exeter streets. Though festive, it was also an intensely patriotic celebration. This tone was set by Thomas D'Alesandro, Jr., as he opined, "Ice cream, to my mind, is a symbol of American living," and was carried to its extreme by Senator Herbert R. O'Conor (D.-Md.), who called the ice cream industry something that could happen only in America, the product of individual initiative and private enterprise, an integral part of the American way of life. Topping it all off, O'Conor exhorted his listeners to "drive away from America the enemies who would destroy these things that make such a centennial possible."

If O'Conor was worried about a Communist assault on ice cream—just the kind of thing that legislators worried about in the 1950s—he could have saved his breath, for ice cream had long before been quietly adopted in the Soviet Union and was flourishing as an adored industry there. The agent for this cultural transfer was Soviet diplomat Anastas Mikoyan, who fell in love with American ice cream in the 1930s and went home to help get an industry started. Today there are seven ice cream plants in Moscow alone, and though ice cream is still uncommon in many parts of the U.S.S.R., the average Muscovite eats more ice cream than the average American.

As it turned out, the American ice cream industry was in for some upheaval, prompted, however, by the vagaries of the capitalistic marketplace, not by any international Communist conspiracy. In fact, as O'Conor spoke, one of the most venerated of all ice cream institutions was being undermined.

SUBVERSION OF THE SODA FOUNTAIN

Although the 1950s saw the industry as a whole doing well, it witnessed a dramatic dropoff in the population of drugstore soda fountains. According to industry sources, fountain removals had reached the rate of 1,200 a year during the early 1950s, while new stores were being planned and built without them. The problem was not lessened consumer demand but stemmed primarily from the advent of hot proprietary items like "wonder drugs," nylon-stocking racks and—perhaps most important— exhaustive lines of cosmetics. From coast to coast beloved Pop's and Doc's opted for bottled miracles and Revlon displays over large, often unprofitable, fountains with their particular breed of "operational problems"—verbal shorthand for such specifics as gum under the counter; Hygeia-straw wrappers dipped, blown, and cemented to the ceiling; un-cost-effective soda jerks; syrup spills; the 3:15 school let-out; drugstore cowboys and rituals like "Mister, can I have another cone? Mine fell on the sidewalk." True to the laws of supply and demand, the slack was picked up elsewhere: custard stands; candy stores; that stainless-steel, formica-and-red-leatherette monument to the era the luncheonette; and, most important, the supermarket.

The fundamental change that was occurring reflected itself

in the statistics. The amount of American ice cream sold in drugstores had gone from 30 percent in 1931 to 14 percent in 1956,
while food-store sales had jumped from 11 to 47 percent of the
sales during the period 1938–1956. The ice cream–marketing
structure had changed: ice cream consumption had shifted from
the fountain to the supermarket. For lovers of good ice cream,
the change was not welcome because the large chain supermarkets, which at first had accepted quality ice creams, soon began
to favor what the trade has come to call "private labels," after
the practice of giving ice cream a house label like "Fro Joy,"
"Blue Ribbon," or "Dutch Treat." In almost every case these
brands pushed the laws of economics and dairy standards to the
limit, combining low cost and high profits, low butterfat and
high overrun (i.e., the air pumped into ice cream to fill the carton). America now had its ice cream *ordinaire* selling for 69
cents the half gallon. In the name of economy, people were starting to buy ice cream so infused with stabilizers and so inflated
with air that it tasted like vanilla (or chocolate) Styrofoam.
This is not to say that there had not been inferior ice creams
before the 1950s, but never before had they been marketed on a
national scale.

Meanwhile, attempts were being made to stem the tide of
defecting fountains and parlors. The trade magazines high-
lighted such widespread but solvable problems as "The Great
Malted Milk Defection," "The Shotgun Menu Mistake," and
"The Abuse of the American Hamburger," while fountain sup-
pliers and trade associations offered upbeat courses in ice cream
parlor management, but to no avail. The defections continued
and the only ice cream coming into many of the new drugstores
was neatly packaged and contained in large self-serve freezers

BORDEN MAIN STREET ICE CREAM PARLOR

MAGIC KINGDOM—WALT DISNEY WORLD

Borden
The elegance of turn-of-the-century Saratoga, New York, is the effect desired in the Borden Main Street Ice Cream Parlor at Disney World near Orlando, Florida. Disneyland in California also boasts an old-fashioned ice cream parlor.

for the take-home market. In 1955 Walt Disney, with the complicity of the Carnation Milk Company, of Los Angeles, opened an "old-fashioned" ice cream parlor at Disneyland in Anaheim. Its opening was an event of symbolic importance signaling the passage of the parlor/fountain from the streetcorner to the realm of the quaint curio. Luckily, however, some of the fountains and parlors were able to buck the tide and they remain today.

The era was not totally devoid of vitality however. On the innovative front were the Dixie Picture Lids with their "Big Name Movie Stars and Cowboys," the Howdy Doody Cake Roll and the Mt. McKinley Ice Cream Company of Fairbanks, Alaska, which pushed its market into the Arctic Circle, claiming to be the first firm selling regularly to the Eskimo. Not to be forgotten were the Humpty-Dumpty episodes which rocked the Yale campus in the spring of 1952. The events stemmed from a series of moves during which the police ordered a mobile Humpty-Dumpty ice cream cart from in front of the campus and reached its zenith in a two-hour riot involving 1,500 students that was quelled with clubs and hoses. Ultimately the vendor, Benjamin Sherman, was allowed to return to the campus and was cheered at a victory rally.

Also emerging during this period was an ice cream folk hero of some proportion. He was the infamous Lawson D. "Two Quart" Butler, who was put on the FBI's "Ten Most Wanted List" in 1952 after he had escaped from the Oregon State Penitentiary where he was serving time for armed robbery. Butler's passion for ice cream was of such strength that he was almost caught in Seattle when a crowd gathered around a drugstore fountain to watch him plow through his well-known portion of two quarts at a sitting. He was able to slip away before FBI agents—alerted by a source aware of Butler's two-quart *modus operandi*—could reach the scene. Later, when the FBI nabbed him in Los Angeles, he was reported to have admitted that he did not mind returning to jail as long as there was ice cream there.

DOMESTIC COLD WAR

The 1950s was the decade in which soda fountains fell by the wayside; the 1960s proved to be the decade in which inefficient plants (many producing marvelous ice cream) and small companies died or were absorbed in droves. U.S. Department of Agriculture figures told of 1,656 plants closing between 1957 and 1969, and as the number of firms grew smaller, entities like Foremost, Beatrice Foods, and Sealtest grew bigger. It was a time of consolidation; the merger and conglomerate instincts were upon the land and small ice cream companies were traded around like so many Popsicle sticks.

Competition was fierce and its results were both good and bad. As the weak, airy supermarket blends became more common some manufacturers responded by creating quality ice creams to carve out a market among those who wanted superior ice cream. To cite one such example, Reuben Mattus, a Bronx manufacturer, had his ice cream frozen out of the supermarket freezer, but rather than go under he turned around and created one of the richest, heaviest, and most expensive ice creams ever to come out of an ice cream plant. He gave it the unsupermarkety name Häagen-Dazs and successfully marketed it in specialty and gourmet shops. (It is in supermarkets now, too.) And as the drugstore soda fountain continued to decline, drugstores started stocking quality ice cream again, but this time to be taken home from their floor freezers. The decade also witnessed the proliferation of a new breed of ice cream parlor/store featuring high-quality ice creams. Some of these were strictly local operations, while others like Baskin-Robbins and Bresler's moved across the land, often reaching the rate of a new store each week.

The picture reveals the same mixture of good and bad for the technology of the 1960s. On one hand, technology gave us many new flavors but, on the other hand, it came up with such abominations as ice cream in an aerosol can (which we can thank test-market consumers in Pennsylvania for rejecting) and space-age ice cream scoops advertised for their ability to avoid "overserving and wasteful skirt." *Skirt* is the term for the extra glob around the base of the ice cream in a cone long known for its ability to produce rivulets of melting ice cream. There was a time when a neat, inviting skirt was the sign of a good scooper.

The result of all of this mixing of good and bad was predictable: the ice cream available ranged from the very good to the very poor.

Meanwhile, on the cultural and political fronts it was an intriguing decade for ice cream. Andy Warhol created a TV ad for Schrafft's featuring the Warhol Sundae portrayed in wavering tones of puce, magenta, chartreuse, and mauve. Three Presidents in a row expressed their love of ice cream, with Richard Nixon going so far as to have his favorite flavor, macadamia nut, flown to the mainland from the Kahala Hilton in Hawaii. Within moments of the Apollo 13 touchdown on the moon, Baskin-Robbins unveiled "Lunar Cheesecake" ice cream in all of its stores while Good Humor rushed "Moon Shot" into its trucks. Sheikh Bader Mulla of Kuwait went to California and bought an ice cream plant which was removed to his country, the Japanese figured out a way to dip ice cream in batter and deep-fry it like tempura, Sealtest successfully moved ice cream in Vienna (something like moving California wine in Paris), and the Swedish government began storing that nation's ice cream surpluses in deep underground caves—suggesting a place for survivors to start a new world order should there ever be thermonuclear war. The era also saw ice cream thrust into a symbolic role for the first time since World War II. In 1963 the New York *Times* and other leading periodicals took to talking about the "Ice Cream Congress." The term was coined in reference to the prevalent opinion that about the only constructive thing the U.S. Congress had done during early 1963 was to repeal a 1921 law that had prohibited the sale of solid milk products in packages of smaller than a half pint in the District of Columbia. Congress, in all its might, had taken the Eskimo Pie and the Dixie Cup off the contraband list, and LBJ signed the bill into law a year later.

All of this brings us to the present, to which we will return in time. But first, with this broad sweep of ice cream history behind us, it is essential that we examine the great phenomena of ice cream. After all, where would ice cream be without the cone, the soda, the float, the sundae. . . .

V

Frozen Assets—The Institutions of Ice Cream

ICE CREAM cannot be fully appreciated in a vacuum; it must be seen in light of the many glorious forms in which it is presented to us. Scant attention has been paid to these edible institutions in the past—unfair, since many of us grew up knowing more than we wanted to know about Eli Whitney and his cotton gin (1793, right?) and nothing about the then more relevant Eskimo Pie or sundae. To rectify this educational injustice, the stories behind some of these lip-smacking institutions have been assembled. Sadly, several defy historical sleuthing and seem to have just appeared around the turn of the century. Such is the case with the ice cream sandwich, the banana split, and the float—and for lack of data the songs of their hero-inventors must go unsung. Fortunately this is not the case with the ice cream soda, the sundae, the cone, and ice cream on a stick.

MR. GREEN'S EXPEDIENT SODA

As is true with almost every worthy ice cream discovery, there is more than one claim to the construction of the first ice cream soda. Unlike other cases, however, the evidence in this one clearly leads us away from a host of pretenders to a Philadelphian who dealt in dispensers of carbonated waters. The other claims—which have come in from such places as Denison, Texas; West Newton, Massachusetts; Omaha; Boston; and Detroit—are normally presented by zealous Chambers of Commerce without any substantial evidence, dates, or names to support them. Most of these spurious claims were run to the ground in the definitive *History of the Soda Fountain Industry* (1947) by Carl J. Palmer (then Executive Secretary of the Soda Fountain Manufacturers Association). Furthermore, Palmer was able to uncover a group of documents, leading us to Philadelphia, which have never been seriously challenged.*

This generally acknowledged creator of the ice cream soda is Robert M. Green, who fathered it in October, 1874, at the semicentennial celebration of the Franklin Institute in Philadelphia, where he was a concessionaire selling soda fountain drinks from a three-foot-square dispenser. At the beginning of the exhibition he was serving a popular drink of the time which was mixture of sweet cream, syrup, and carbonated water. During

* Since Palmer's research was conducted only one new contender of note has emerged. It is Baur's, a Denver ice cream parlor, which claimed in a 1968 issue of *Gourmet* magazine that its Otto Baur first served an ice cream soda in 1871—three years before Green. However, since Baur's has chosen not to answer the author's request for substantiating evidence, the claim must be written off with others of its unsupported ilk.

Part of James W. Tufts' gargantuan soda fountain at the Centennial Exhibition of 1876 in Philadelphia. Tufts gambled most of his resources on the huge two-story fountain and the palatial building that housed it, but later reported that it had been ''successful beyond all expectation.'' The ornate soda fountain had gotten a tremendous publicity boost, and a year later the new Tufts catalog featured no less than fifty fountains of great variety in design.

one of the early days of the celebration, however, he ran out of cream and began substituting vanilla ice cream. The customers gave their hearty approval to the new drink as evidenced by the fact that Green, who had been averaging $6 a day with the first drink, was taking in over $600 a day for ice cream sodas by the end of the exhibition. Green went on to make a fortune as a soda manufacturer, and when he died in 1920 his will called for a large monument to be erected over his grave with the inscription: ORIGINATOR OF THE ICE CREAM SODA. His firm, Robt. M. Green and Sons, continued to flourish until after World War II, when national priorities turned against the amenity of the soda fountain.

Two years after Green's soda first appeared, it had become such a sensation that James W. Tufts, another pioneer soda fountain manufacturer, paid $50,000 for the sole right to dispense ice cream sodas at the Philadelphia Centennial which was held to commemorate the one hundredth anniversary of the Declaration of Independence.* By 1893 an American magazine had heralded the ice cream soda as "the national beverage" and it was being served in every corner of the land. Similarly, by 1892 the ice cream soda had clearly moved across the Atlantic, for in that year a British analytical chemist named G. H. Dubelle had published his *Soda Fountain Beverages,* which contained a formula-laden chapter on the new drink.

In no time at all the ice cream soda became a fresh new men-

---

* The dispenser brought by Tufts was described this way in the Boston *Journal of Commerce:* "It will be over thirty feet in height, with an open interior which can be reached by descending into the cellar and ascending the stairs on the inside. The lower story, or section, of the apparatus is devoted to soda water, syrups, ice etc.; the second story will be occupied by a beautiful fountain, playing perfumed waters, surrounded by rare exotics, ferns and flowers; while the upper story, surmounted by a handsome dome and staff with the banner of 'Arctic Soda' floating therefrom, will be illuminated from the interior by an elegant chandelier."

ace for the more excitable members of the American clergy. As Stewart H. Holbrook observes in his *Lost Men of American History:* "In the author's native town of Newport, Vermont, as late as 1890, a powerful sermon was preached against 'sucking soda' and eating ice cream in drugstores on the Sabbath; and in certain Midwest towns laws were passed against the abomination, and the selling of soda water on Sunday was prohibited." Such actions begged for another fountain concoction—one that would be so constructed as to skirt the intolerant Sunday blue laws legally.

THE SEVENTH-DAY CONCOCTION

It becomes apparent to the ice cream researcher that Chambers of Commerce and Sunday-supplement writers are not historians and are prone to traffic in the apocryphal, especially if it has a local angle. Consequently, just as there are scads of local claims on the ice cream soda, so there are scads more on the sundae—and it would be futile to try to list all the communities insisting that they be honored as the birthplace of the sundae.

Sifting out the chaff, these facts remain. The ice cream sundae emerged in the late 1890s and became extremely popular around the turn of the century. This popularity was substantially aided by laws prohibiting the sale of sodas on Sunday, and for this reason the concoction was first known as the "Sunday" or the "Soda-less Soda." The more elegant *-ae* ending probably came about when those who orated from the pulpit on the sinful soda went to work on the sacrilegious use of the name of the Sabbath for its stand-in.

As for the specific birthplace of the dish, two possibilities emerge as the most likely among many contenders. Neither place can offer conclusive dates, so one can pick between "Heavenston" (favored by the National Dairy Council, among others) and Two Rivers (championed by such diverse sources as the old *Ice Cream Review* and H. L. Mencken in his *American Language*).

The first claim goes back to the 1890s in Evanston, Illinois (then widely known as "Chicago's Heaven" or "Heavenston"), where civic piety had reached such a state that it became the first American community to recognize and legislate against the "Sunday Soda Menace." This prompted confectioners to create Sundays so that they could do business on the Sabbath. Ironically the soda was later given a strong boost from this community when the Evanston-based Women's Christian Temperance Union (WCTU) championed it as a pleasant alternative to alcoholic drinks.

The Two Rivers, Wisconsin, claim goes back to the same era and, so the story goes, was created when a youth named George Hallauer went into Ed Berner's soda fountain for a dish of ice cream. As the ice cream was being scooped, the daring Hallauer spied a bottle of chocolate syrup normally used in sodas and asked Berner to pour some of it over his ice cream. Berner sampled the concoction and liked it enough to begin featuring "ice cream with syrup" in his shop for the same price as a dish of ice cream. The name *sundae* was given to the dish when George Giffy, an ice cream parlor proprietor in nearby Manitowoc, was forced by customer demand to serve the popular Berner concoction. Giffy was convinced that the nickel dish would put him out of business and at first served it only as a Sunday loss leader. In Manitowoc it soon became known as "the Sunday." Giffy soon found that he was making money on the dish and began advertising his "Ice Cream Sundaes," with the spelling changed so that it would lose its Sunday-only association.

Regardless of the origin, by 1900, midwestern soda-fountain supply salesmen were carrying samples of tulip-shaped "Sundae Specials." Within a few more years they would be carrying an even hotter new item: the World's Fair Cornucopia, later known as the ice cream cone.

THE SOMEWHAT CONFUSING SAGA OF THE ICE CREAM CONE

On April 28, 1954, the pooh-bahs of the cone and ice cream industries assembled in St. Louis to celebrate the golden anniversary of the ice cream cone. Under the sponsorship of the International Association of Ice Cream Manufacturers (IAICM), the two-day celebration/convention was held at the Chase Hotel, built atop the very spot where the Association had determined that the first cone had been made.

It was a festive affair honoring the late Ernest A. Hamwi, a Syrian who had come to St. Louis from Damascus in 1903. Based on the IAICM's investigations, the birth of the cone goes like this. In 1904 the St. Louis' Exposition—also known as the St. Louis World's Fair and the Louisiana Purchase Exposition— opened and Hamwi obtained a concession there to sell zalabia, a crisp waferlike Persian pastry baked on a flat waffle iron and served with sugar and other sweets. Close to Hamwi's stand was an ice cream concessionaire who was selling his product in 5-and-10-cent dishes. One extremely busy day, the ice cream stand ran out of dishes and the alert Hamwi rolled one of his wafers into a cornucopia, let it cool, and put a scoop of ice cream in its mouth. The ice cream vendor was intrigued with the idea and the "World's Fair Cornucopia" was born. It was an immediate hit at the Fair.

This version of the birth of the cone was confirmed by Association research, the testimony of Hamwi's relatives, and the eyewitness account of Stephen H. Sullivan who, as a young man, had been at the Fair and witnessed the historic marriage of waffle and ice cream. The Hamwi story became the official version and news of it was carried across the land by the press.

During the very year that the cone anniversary was being celebrated, the New York *Times* carried the obituary of Italo Marchiony, an Italian immigrant who until his death had pushed to advance his claim as inventor of the cone. Ironically it was his obituary that brought him to public attention. The *Times* article, which appeared on October 29, 1954, stated that Marchiony had been making cones and selling them as early as 1896 and that he applied for a patent on his cone mold, which was issued on December 13, 1904—well before the Fair opened. The mold was described in the patent application as being "split in two like a waffle iron and producing several small round pastry cups with sloping sides."

Marchiony's obituary appeared a scant twenty-five days after a *Times* article on the fiftieth anniversary of the cone that gave credit to Hamwi. Besides correcting itself, the *Times* had challenged the International Association and the *National Geographic,* to name a few. Others joined in the row and, to cite one, the Washington *Post* sided with Marchiony after talking with Peter Marchiony, Italo's son, and checking again with the patent office.

Since the Marchiony-Hamwi row of 1954 at least two other contenders have emerged. In 1965 another *Times* obituary brought the name David Avayou into the contest. The *Times* reported that Avayou, a native of Turkey and long-time operator of a string of Atlantic City, New Jersey, ice cream shops, had long claimed to have invented the cone while working at the St. Louis Fair. He claimed that he had first seen cones in France, where ice cream was eaten from *paper* cones, and had applied the idea in edible form at the Fair. Even more recently the name of Abe Doumar has been introduced into the controversy. The Doumar claim has been advanced via a paper (and a set of photographs) written and circulated by his son, Al. The mimeographed monograph, entitled *The Saga of the Ice Cream Cone,* had an immediate impact in ice cream circles. *The Western Ice Cream News* went so far as to tout the revisionist document in a 1971 article entitled ''The Ice Cream Cone Revisited.'' The Doumar version begins with Abe Doumar and a partner leaving their home in North Bergen, New Jersey, to hawk Holy Land souvenirs at a section of the St. Louis Exposition called the Old City of Jerusalem. At the Fair, their hottest item was a 50-cent glass paperweight filled with ''Jordan River Water.'' According to the Doumar manuscript, the cone was born as follows: ''The 'Jerusalem Streets' closed daily at 6:00 P.M. but the entertainment section stayed open until the crowds thinned. A certain waffle shop was the gathering place for the workers and concessionaires. Nightly, Abe could be found there chatting with other Syrians and Lebanese. . . . One night at the waffle stand, Abe took one of the French waffles in much the same way as he would have taken the top part of a round Syrian loaf and rolled it up to form a scoop or horn. He went next door and put some ice cream in it and told the waffle man that this would increase both the sales of waffles and his gross per unit sale. The waffle man told him to be his guest and try it out. This Abe did nightly, after 6:00 P.M. They called them Cornucopias and sold them with success. The waffle man was delighted and gave Abe one of the waffle irons to take home with him at the end of the season.''

Muddying these waters even more are the claims that have come in from overseas. Travelers had reported eating ice cream from edible containers in Düsseldorf years before the Fair, and in nineteenth-century France ice cream was known to have been eaten from paper and metal cones. What is more, research conducted by the author has yielded still another possibility. An August, 1947, Chicago *Sun* feature story tells of Max Goldberg, then chairman of the board of that cone-giant, the Illinois Baking Company, who was described as a cone pioneer who ''fretted over it, nursed it along, ate it, sold it and developed it over 44 years into a big manufacturing business.'' Goldberg told the *Sun* that he had first sold cones in 1903. He bought the cones from an unnamed Brooklyn firm that had started making them in 1902.

All of this is not easy to sort out. Even such august groups as the Missouri Historical Society have thrown up their hands in desperation. It would appear, however, that the Marchiony patent wins for him the credit as American inventor of the ice cream cone, but since he never achieved any success or popularity with his invention the distinction of introducing it to a waiting America goes to a group of men—which one is not sure—at the St. Louis Fair of 1904. Since records indicate that there were at least fifty ice cream booths at the Fair (collectively dispensing 5,000 gallons on good days) and almost as many waffle stands, it is conceivable that historic marriages of waffle and ice cream occurred independently at several spots on the grounds. (However, despite this wealth of contradictory evidence, many sources—ranging from major encyclopedias to the *National Geographic*—have long since decided that Hamwi gets full credit. So it goes in the history-writing business.)

The cone gained popularity quickly. Before the Fair was over, St. Louis foundries were banging out baking molds for making the World's Fair Cornucopia, and those who played a part in its introduction fanned out to popularize and profit from the novelty. Avayou took the cone to Philadelphia where he set up a concession in a department store. Hamwi went on to run the Cornucopia Waffle Company and later founded the Missouri Cone Company. At the time of the cone demi-centennial in 1954 his nephew was still in the cone business in St. Louis. Sullivan became a cone dealer, first selling them at something called the Modern Woodmen of America Frisco Log Rolling in Sullivan, Missouri. Doumar went back to New Jersey and produced a cone oven and opened the first of his many ice cream cone stands at Coney Island in 1905. He later moved to such locations as the Jamestown Exposition of 1907 and brought the cone to major resorts all along the East Coast. For a while he manufactured cones but, according to his son, that business went under when the giant National Biscuit Company entered the field with a cut-rate cone.* Finally, a young Ohio State engineering student who had been taken with the cone at the Fair perfected an automatic cone-rolling machine, which he introduced in 1909.

The ice cream cone industry developed rapidly, and in 1924

---

* Abe Doumar's last ice cream stand was opened in 1934 at the corner of 20th and Monticello streets in Norfolk, Virginia. "Doumars" in Norfolk is in operation to this day and is run by Abe's two sons, who still feature cones.

The Bettmann Archive
As these society matrons illustrate, the cone had become an American institution in just a few years. In 1924, twenty years after it had been introduced, America wolfed down an estimated 245 million of them.

an estimated 245 million of them were produced. The competition to create best-seller cone designs became fierce.

Such was competition in the cone business by the 1930s that companies would bring out a new line each year. The Turnbull Cone Company, for example, ran ads reading "Turnbull's Cones for 1935" which featured pictures of such ornate new models as "Royalty," "Big Head," "Baby Grand," and "Gold Leaf." The burden of this intense activity fell on the U.S. Patent Office, which had to pass on the hundreds of applications for variations on the basic theme. Each issue of *The Ice Cream Review* carried a section on new cones along with little sketches in the style of Leonardo da Vinci's *Notebook* designs. Many of these were only flamboyant embellishments on the basic design, while others were ingenious examples of micro-engineering. There were cones with a side-pouch for an extra scoop, spiral cones, cones that stood on the table, those that looked like rocket ships (or Gothic spires), those that borrowed from turn-of-the-century bathtub designs, and "dripless" models of every description. One of these drip-less cones contained an elaborate system of annular troughs while another featured a patented built-in candy catch-basin.

This decade-long flurry of intense creative activity, when inventors throughout the land dreamed of originating *the* great American cone, is half-forgotten history today. Several major cone companies emerged to dominate, and today all we are offered from them is a basic cake-and-sugar cone, with a few minor variations from firm to firm. Form now follows function to the letter, and there are no longer new-model years and creative touches. The cone has become the Volkswagen of the ice cream world. But do not let this trend to simplicity obscure a great virtue of the cone. As an environmentally concerned Department of Health, Education and Welfare official said on television recently: "The ice cream cone is the only ecologically sound package known. It is the perfect package."

THE STICKY TRIUMVIRATE

Taken together the Eskimo Pie, the Good Humor bar, and the Popsicle have had a tremendous impact on the ice cream industry. When they were developed they gave the industry an immediate shot in the arm and helped it mitigate the effects of the depression. Although early in their histories they fought each other in vicious patent squabbles, they coexist today and are the dominant novelties, as the industry calls them, of the market. All three were invented between 1919 and 1924 and there has not been a significant new ice cream novelty since. Presented in chronological order, here are the presto-and-eureka stories behind them.

One afternoon in 1919 a young boy entered a candy store in Onawa, Iowa, and ordered an ice cream sandwich but then changed his mind and ordered a candy bar. Christian Nelson, the proprietor, asked the boy if he really knew what he wanted, to which he replied, "Sure I know—I want 'em both, but I only got a nickel." The lad's comment prompted Nelson, a Danish-born schoolteacher who ran the candy store as a sideline, to conclude that there was probably a market for a confection that combined chocolate candy with ice cream. He experimented with the idea but got nowhere because he was unable to make chocolate stick to ice cream. Weeks later he learned from a candy salesman that cocoa butter improves the clinging ability of chocolate, and he

tried again. He succeeded on the first try and dubbed his choco-
late-covered creation the ''I-Scream Bar.'' The first five hundred
bars were taken to the Onawa Firemen's Tournament, and all
were sold.

Convinced that his was a money-making creation, Nelson
applied for a patent and set out to sell it in Omaha. In 1921, after
months of failure during which he was reduced to racking balls
in a pool hall for $20 a week, he met an Omaha ice cream company
superintendent named Russell Stover who liked the idea, and a
partnership was established. Stover felt that there must be a
better name for the confection than ''I-Scream'' and he came up
with ''Eskimo Pie,'' which he thought had more commercial ap-
peal. The early Eskimo Pie, a small 1½-ounce stickless bar, was
introduced during the summer of 1921 in Des Moines, where it
was an immediate sensation. In Omaha later in the same summer,
Stover and Nelson put a quarter of a million bars on the market
and they were all sold within twenty-four hours. A national office was set up in Chicago and area franchises sold like so many
Eskimo Pies. In less than a year over 1,500 licenses to make the
pies had been issued.*

By the spring of 1922 sales were averaging a million pies a
day and Nelson, who was collecting $30,000 a week in royalties,
was being compared to Horatio Alger's most meteoric heroes.
But just as the pie took off and the money started rolling in,
problems emerged, and by 1923 the company was fast going
broke. Those who wanted more than their fair share of the pie

* As is true of almost every significant ice cream innovation, the origin of the
Eskimo Pie has been challenged. One Ralph A. Lee long claimed to have beaten
Nelson to the punch but if he did he never took it to the patent office. Lee, however,
is not without a niche in ice cream history; he was the first to manufacture a thermal
bag to keep ice cream cold. Lee once sent ice cream packed in one of the bags to President Woodrow Wilson to prove dramatically the effectiveness of his invention.

Eskimo Pie Corp.
Delivery man restocking Eskimo Pie Thermos Dispenser in 1929.
Chris Nelson, the man who invented the Pie, developed this Dry
Ice dispenser to get ice cream out of store refrigerators onto the
countertop to promote impulse buying.

were not paying royalties, and dozens of imitators freely infringed on the patent. The company was spending $4,000 a day to defend the patent. Stover became so upset by the situation that he sold his share to Nelson for $30,000 and went on to Denver where he used that money to open the first Russell Stover Candy Store. Meanwhile Nelson went looking for help and found it in R. S. Reynolds, who ran the U.S. Foil Company, which is today known as Reynolds Metals. It was a natural combination, since Reynolds's company was working around the clock to produce the gleaming foil wrappers for the Eskimo Pie, and Reynolds had told Nelson on their first meeting, "Young man, I've just made a million dollars on your idea." In 1924 they merged and Eskimo Pie became a U.S. Foil subsidiary. Thereafter, Nelson, who did not enjoy marketing chores, concentrated on research.

By the time Nelson retired from Reynolds in 1961, he had run up an impressive record as an innovator. Upon hearing about solidified carbon dioxide, or Dry Ice, Nelson got in touch with its inventors and pioneered in using it to ship ice cream—a move that made ice cream infinitely more shippable and led to a shift in the industry from local to regional plants. He invented the "Eskimo Jug," a thermos dispenser that brought the pie to places that could not afford refrigerated cabinets, and the "Eskimo Machine," an ice cream extruder capable of 7,200 pies an hour. Today Nelson still forwards new ideas to the company from his place of retirement in California.

Although the Eskimo Pie patent was declared invalid in 1928, the company kept a large share of the market and prospers today. Latest word from its headquarters (the Eskimo Building in Richmond, Virginia) is that 750 million pies are being sold annually. There are Eskimo Pie factories in Luxembourg, England, France, and Canada, and expansion into Japan, Holland, and Australia is anticipated.

One of those who heard of Nelson's original 1919 discovery that melted chocolate could be made to adhere to ice cream was Harry Burt, a confectioner and ice cream parlor operator in Youngstown, Ohio. Burt, who had successfully marketed a lollipop called the Good Humor Sucker, was always looking for new ideas, so in 1920 he decided to try to replicate Nelson's feat. After a series of failures, late one night Burt emerged from his hardening room and presented his new ice cream bar to the family to taste. His daughter approved but thought the bar "too messy" and asked why he did not put it on a stick like his famous lollipop. Father Burt went back to the hardening room and tried a new prototype model with a stick in it. A bond was formed by ice crystals interlocking with the wooden handle and it stuck. He immediately applied for a patent on the Good Humor Ice Cream Sucker. Burt liked the name "Good Humor" because it expressed his belief that the humors of the mind were regulated by those of the palate.

After three years of waiting, the Good Humor patent had still not come through, so Burt's son, Harry, Jr., was sent to Washington with a five-gallon can of Good Humors which he carried to the Patent Office. Young Harry literally forced his evidence into the mouths of patent officials, who then agreed that it was an original idea and granted the patent.

Before the patent was issued the Burt family had begun selling Good Humors. Harry, Sr., convinced that his unique product needed unique marketing, outfitted a white truck with a set of bells (from the family bobsled) and dressed the driver in

Eskimo Pie Corp.

Eskimo Pie trucks preparing to roll from the Brooklyn factory in the late 1920s. C. K. Nelson, the man who invented the Eskimo Pie, was the first to use Dry Ice to ship ice cream—a development that allowed ice cream to be hauled over longer distances, thereby changing the industry from one of small local plants to large regional ones.

white. Soon there were a dozen of these trucks jingling around Youngstown. The Good Humor was a local success with potential as a national product, so in 1926, when Harry Burt died, all rights to the Good Humor were quickly snatched up by a group of Cleveland businessmen who formed The Good Humor Corp. of America. Their idea was to sell Good Humor franchises for a $100 down payment. A young Tennesseean, Tom Brimer, bought a group of these franchises, opened first (and prospered) in Detroit, and then went on to Chicago.

One of the early breaks for Good Humor came at the hands of mobsters. No sooner had Brimer opened his operation in Chicago in 1929 than he was issued the then-common ultimatum of "$5,000 for protection"—or else. Brimer ignored the demand but did increase the insurance on his equipment. A few days later eight Good Humor trucks were blown up. The cost was covered by insurance and the explosions put Good Humor on the front pages, with the result that sales shot up. At the end of 1929—a bad time for things financial—Brimer paid his stockholders a very impressive 25 percent dividend.

This dividend attracted the attention of a Wall Street speculator named Michael J. Meehan, who had bought some shares in Brimer's operation based on a tip. Meehan was so impressed that he called Brimer to New York and after consulting with him told him to go to Cleveland and secure national rights to the Good Humor. Meehan paid close to $500,000 and acquired a 75 percent share of the company.

As it quickly evolved, the company took on a distinct caste with strong paramilitary overtones. It kept tight reign on its flotillas of spotless vans and its white-uniformed troops, with their shiny Sam Browne belts, who, in the 1930s, were required

Good Humor Corporation
A typical New York area Good Humor branch operation on the first day of
the season, with the troops assembled for a traditional portrait.

to raise their caps to women customers and issue snappy salutes to men. Such was the discipline, reported *Business Week* in 1932, that the man who said, "Good Humor ice cream" instead of the official "Ice cream Good Humor" might find himself drummed out of the corps. To stay in line, drivers studied their manual, *Making Good with Good Humor,* which not only contained stern rules but paternalistic advice—a sample: "Eat regularly at a good restaurant with your mind free from worry. . . ."

Another characteristic of the company was its shrewd approach to free publicity. For example, Good Humor's man in California made sure that trucks were always parked outside Hollywood radio stations and movie studios. The result was steady mention on the radio (Said the late Fred Allen, "Ripley knows a cannibal chief with a sweet tooth—for dessert he always eats a Good Humor man."), roll-on roles in over one hundred motion pictures during the 1930s and 1940s, and star billing in Columbia's *The Good Humor Man.* But a lot of the free publicity did not have to be prompted because, like the Fuller Brush man, the Good Humor man was a distinct American institution. When he appeared early in the year, newspapers ran his picture with the caption: FIRST SIGN OF SPRING. Cartoonists loved him so much that eventually it was possible to publish an anthology of Good Humor cartoons. Magazine cover illustrators and comedians loved him too. ("Hear about the man who crashed into a playground fence? Thought he was following a white line, actually it was a Good Humor truck leaking vanilla.")

Although long beset with legal problems ranging from its defense of the Good Humor patent (which finally ran out right after World War II) to formal antinoise complaints (the most prestigious of which was drawn up for a bell-bedeviled Jascha

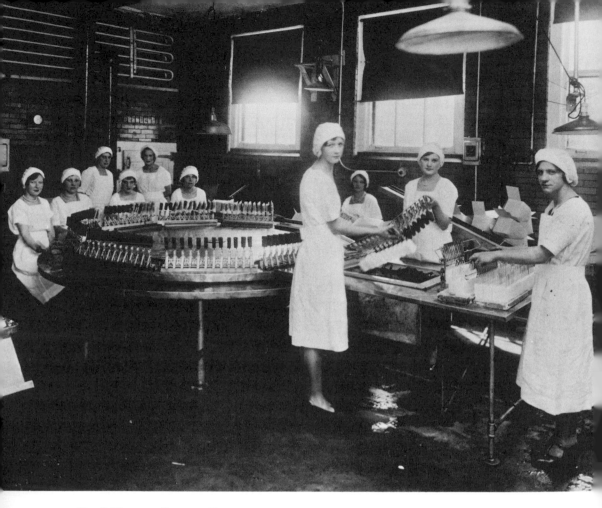

Good Humor Corporation
The late 1920s were modern times to these Good Humor ladies who hand dipped the ice cream in chocolate and hand packed the bars into wrappers— a process long since mechanized.

Heifetz by his lawyer), the company has always done well and has never had any truly close national competition in mobile vending.* In 1961, when the conglomerate movement was beginning in earnest, Good Humor was picked up by Thomas J. Lipton Inc. and thrown into the hopper with that company's mix of tea, soups, and salad dressings.

The third member of the great novelty triumvirate of the 1920s was born on a cold eureka-shouting morning in New Jersey in 1923. The inventor was Frank Epperson, who made lemonade from a specially prepared powder that he sold at an Oakland, California, amusement park. While visiting friends in New Jersey, he prepared a batch of special lemonade and inadvertently left a glass of it on a windowsill with a spoon in it. The temperature went down below zero during the night and in the morning Epperson saw the glass. He picked it up by the spoon handle and ran hot water over the glass freeing the frozen mass. In his hand was the first Epsicle, later to be known as the Popsicle. Epperson saw immediately the potential of what he held in his hand and applied for a patent, which was granted in 1924. He was fortunate, because research conducted by *The Ice Cream Review* in 1925 revealed that a major ice cream company was experimenting with "frozen suckers" at the time of the windowsill incident, and as far back as 1872 two men doing business as Ross and Robbins sold a frozen-fruit confection on a stick, which they called the Hokey-Pokey.

Epperson later sold his patent to the Joe Lowe Corporation

---

* One ruling which went against Good Humor was the celebrated "Lucky Sticks" case. For years the company branded one out of twelve sticks a "Lucky Stick" which entitled the lucky finder to a free Good Humor. In 1938 the Federal Trade Commission ruled the custom "an illegal lottery," a move that prompted more than one editorial writer to suggest that bureaucracy did not know the difference between criminality and good fun.

1922

International Association of Ice Cream Manufacturers
This 1922 photograph of a Baltimore hokey-pokey man and his clients under-
scores the point that "old-fashioned" ice cream often left something to be
desired when it came to sanitary considerations. In city after city the hokey-
pokey carts disappeared after public health officials banned them.

(now called Popsicle Industries), which went on to create the Twin Popsicle, Creamsicle, and other members of the Sicle family. Today three billion of these products are made each year, hammered out in more than four hundred ice cream plants.

Since the brief period during which Nelson, Burt, and Epperson sent their patent applications to Washington, there have been thousands of discoveries and inventions in the world of ice cream, but most of them have been either variations on earlier themes or technical advances (which, we shall see, is not always an advance in the direction of better ice cream). Ranged alongside such creations as the cone, the ice cream soda, the sundae, and the ice-cream-on-a-stick family, they are minor. In fact, what may be the most significant development since the discovery of ice cream itself predates the discoveries covered in this chapter and goes back to the laboratory of Joseph Priestley and to an enthusiastic early-nineteenth-century American named John Matthews. Through them the soda fountain emerged.

VI

Jerks and Bubble Merchants

NATURALLY carbonated waters have forever been seeping up from the ground, offending animals and causing humans to build resorts around them. The first recorded instance of man himself carbonating water came in 1767 when Joseph Priestley, the English Unitarian divine and discoverer of oxygen, created a glass of it in his laboratory by charging water with carbonic-acid gas collected from brewery vats in Leeds. Other scientists of the era experimented with the process and then, in 1770, Swedish chemist Torbern Bergman pushed the Priestley discovery one step further by coming up with a means of producing carbonic-acid gas in commercial quantities. It remained something of a laboratory curiosity until the beginning of the next century in the United States where several forward-looking scientists began to see its commercial possibilities. Benjamin Silliman, Yale University's first professor of chemistry, began bottling and selling it around New York in 1807 and a year later Dr. Philip S. Physick, the University of Pennsylvania's first professor of surgery, added minerals to carbonated water and began selling it. By 1810 in New York City it was selling briskly as a cure for obesity.

THE FOUNTAIN'S YOUTH

It was not until 1832 when young John Matthews arrived in New York from England to seek his fortune that carbonated water became an industry of consequence. Matthews knew how to make carbonic-acid gas and reasoned that there was a market for such a skill in New York. He began by supplying carbonated water to New York stores, where it was consumed cold and straight, and then he began manufacturing a compact dog-house-sized apparatus for carbonating water which was soon widely known as the fountain. In time several others entered the field—including such soon-to-be-giants of the field as A. D. Puffer of Boston and John Lippincott of Philadelphia—and an industry was born to supply America with straight, unembellished seltzer.

Matthews was a soda booster of the first order and helped to popularize seltzer water in America through his own prose. He wrote in one of his catalogs: "Youth as it sips its first soda experiences the sensations of which, like the sensations of love, cannot be forgotten but cherished to the last." And in another advertisement claimed: ". . . nearly all physicians are consumers of this beverage. Among the most civilized and cultivated of mankind, its consumption is rapidly increasing."

The New-York Historical Society
After many years of intense design competition, which produced such flamboyant originals as the Puffer Commonwealth of 1889, the four largest soda fountain manufacturers merged into one in 1894. As Tufts, Puffer, Lippincott and Matthews became the American Soda Fountain Co., the great design race slowed considerably.

Besides contributing to the growing literature of bombastic claims for carbonated water, Matthews advanced the art of soda-making. He pioneered in new ways of producing the needed carbonic-acid gas and was the first to liberate it by mixing sulfuric acid and marble chips. Matthews's firm secured the rights to picking up the scrap marble produced by the construction of St. Patrick's Cathedral in New York, which in itself was enough to carbonate twenty-five million gallons of water.

In addition to Matthews and other manufacturers there were others who had a profound influence on the development of the fountain. One was a French immigrant who in 1825 opened the first "modern" drugstore at the corner of Sixth and Chestnut streets in Philadelphia. He was Elié Magliore Durand, a pharmacist in Napoleon's army, who correctly reasoned that the American pharmacy was ready for a new incarnation. Not only did his store have an entire glass front and feature mirrors, marble-topped counters and mahogany display cases, but he sold cigars and featured soda water—the first to appear in a drugstore. National attention was focused on Durand's unique drugstore when Lafayette, then on a triumphal tour of America, stopped in Philadelphia to see two old friends: Joseph Bonaparte, Napoleon's brother, and Durand. This first corner drugstore in the modern sense quickly became a center for the physicians, scientists, and literati of Philadelphia who were drawn there by the combination of sparkling water and the erudite and well-connected Durand.

The next person to have seminal influence on the fountain was another Frenchman immigrating to Philadelphia. Eugène Roussel, a perfume dealer who sold soda in his shop, was the first to make the connection between soda and syrups, and in 1838 or

The Transcendent.

The New-York Historical Society
The Transcendent is one of thirty-one similarly elaborate fountains offered in the 1879 catalog of A. D. Puffer and Sons of Boston. One distinct feature of the Puffer fountains was that each came with a hose which could be attached to convert it into what Puffer called "the best fire annihilator ever made."

1839 began adding flavors to his soda. The idea spread quickly and within a few years it was common for a soda fountain owner to carry an arsenal of syrups, normally including such fashionable flavors as birch beer, pepsin, ginger, lemon, kola, cherry, sarsaparilla, champagne, and claret. The result of the perfumer's discovery was the establishment of a much larger market for carbonated water.

Next to make his mark on the fountain was Gustavus D. Dows, of Lowell, Massachusetts, the first to bring marble and other ornate touches to the normally drab apparatus of soda dispensing. In 1858 Dows first offered a small cottage-shaped combination fountain and ice shaver in a white Italian marble housing for $225. We know little more about this Cellini of the fountain than that he did a brisk business in Boston and was successful enough to exhibit his fountain in Paris. Dows's influence was nonetheless great, for he touched off interest in the fountain as an artful object. Though Dows's small "cottage" fountains were models of cool restraint, his followers soon lapsed into the ultra-ornate, embellishing their fountains with such items as cathedral spires, Doric columns, gargoyle spigots, sphinxes, and goddesses. Often the total object was a hodgepodge of allegorical reference set in an awkward stew of decorative styles.*

Finally, Robert Green came along and gave the industry the ice cream soda, which served to bring ice cream to more soda

---

* Perhaps the best example of the soda fountain style of the last half of the nineteenth century is not a fountain per se but the fountainlike granite monument which rises aboves the mortal remains of John Matthews in Greenwood Cemetery, Brooklyn. Constructed in the Matthews's workshop after his death in 1870, the mausoleum features a richly carved thirty-six-foot-high canopy over a likeness of Matthews. The canopy houses a collection of carved images ranging from mythological beasts to bas-relief scenes illuminating great moments in the life of the nation's most influential seltzer man.

fountains. For a while it had been common for druggists to store and sell ice cream from the ice compartment of their fountains; with the advent of the ice cream soda it became all but obligatory.

A MARBLE TO BEHOLD

In 1903 a new fountain came on the market. It did not stand against the wall but was actually a counter which one could stand behind, there to work with an array of draft arms, syrup pumps, and deep ice-packed wells containing ice cream. The first of these was installed at the Broad Street Pharmacy in Philadelphia, and within a few years hardly a town in America was without a modern fountain. Although not as ornate as earlier models, the new fountains did not skimp when it came to fine materials and elegant trappings like glass umbrella-shaped lampshades, sculpted light standards, and fine glassware. However, the counter itself was the center of attraction and many a corner druggist went into debt to compete with a white Italian marble, alabaster, black slate, or Mexican onyx fountain top.

As styles changed and technical developments came along, the fountain changed, although never radically, and by the 1920s it was a well-entrenched full-fledged American institution. It was the social, if not cultural, center of numerous small towns, and many a footnote to twentieth-century American history was created in it. For instance, over sodas at Robinson's Drugstore in Dayton, Tennessee, on May 5, 1923, a young teacher named John Thomas Scopes was persuaded by a freethinking businessman to test publicly the state's ban on teaching "theories that deny the divine creation of man." Later, after the Scopes trial

THE object of this engraving is, that persons not familiar with soda-water apparatus may understand what is necessary for the manufacture and dispensing of soda-water. Of course, the generator and fountains may be omitted if desired, where the charged water can be bought of a dealer in that line.

The New-York Historical Society
A descriptive illustration from the 1885 catalog of the Jas. W. Tufts Co. Tufts was a Massachusetts druggist who became the leading fountain manufacturer of the 1880s. Among his many accomplishments was that he bought the land, founded and built the town of Pinehurst, North Carolina, which became a famous winter resort for golfers.

began, Robinson's became the meeting place for the likes of H. L. Mencken and Clarence Darrow.*

During the 1920s and into the 1930s the fountains being built were no less artful than their predecessors. Fountain-building was spurred by Prohibition as many a hotel and cocktail lounge converted their bars to fountains for the duration. In *Playboy* style, *Soda Fountain* magazine devoted its centerfold to the great new fountains of the era as they came on the line. Many were huge by any standard. In back-to-back issues of 1932 the magazine featured the fashionable 800-seat Broadmoor fountain on Madison Avenue and the gargantuan 1,200-seat fountain built into Chicago's Merchandise Mart. Others were featured for reasons of style rather than size, such as the ersatz Louis XIV fountain in the Ambassador Hotel in Los Angeles, Gilchrist's Marble Spa in Boston—as much a museum of rare alabasters and marbles as a fountain—and Bullard's in Chicago, a 97-foot-long display of ornate tilework.

The flamboyance of the new fountains was matched only by the creations being served in them. Such was the fervor of concocting in 1932 that a guest editorial by an ice cream manufacturer appeared in *Soda Fountain* protesting the "Hodge Podge at the Fountain." Alluding to such excesses as "The Flapper's Experience" and the "Chocolate Enchilada" (many of which were being promulgated in the magazine) the author said, "They disrupt my mental digestion and arise to haunt me with terrible potentialities. I freeze in vari-colored gobs of ice cream; smother

---

* After the trial Scopes, who was found guilty but freed on a technicality, went back to teaching and consuming ice cream sodas, which he had a particular passion for. Robinson's declined into the kind of tourist trap with "See Where It All Started" signs cluttering the roads of the area and a full line of "Monkey Trial" souvenirs (like a key chain with an ape's head attached).

in oodles of whipped cream; wallow in oozy marshmallow. Floods of syrup engulf me. I am bombarded with pecans, walnuts and peanuts. I seem to become at one with them."

Often appreciation of this distinctly American institution came from overseas observers, who were not jaded by their bedazzling qualities by virtue of the fact that they had not grown up among them. As Sir John Fraser wrote in the London *Standard* in 1920:

> These parlors—I leave the "u" out of the word in deference to my American friends—are really gorgeous establishments.
>
> They are spacious, scrupulously clean, and decorative. On one side is a long white marble counter, and you sit on a high stool whilst white-clad young men spryly supply the thirsty mob.
>
> There is grape juice and logan berry juice, root beer, orangeade, coco-cola [*sic*], cherry phosphate, lime-ade, mixtures of aerated water, ice cream, crushed strawberries, chocolate sundaes, and ice cream of many colors and many flavors. There are thousands of these places. . . .
>
> At the rear part of the establishment are nice glass covered tables, where you can sit and while the hours away consuming inordinate quantities of iced soft drinks and listening to a band, or a nickel in the slot machine, not infrequently a horrible but ingenious German contrivance of a fiddle played by electricity. . . .
>
> Young people do not go for country walks in America. They chiefly consort in the ice cream parlors. . . .

The fountain continued to grow and prosper right through the 1940s, and at the end of that ice-cream-gorging year of 1946 the Soda Fountain Manufacturers Association in Chicago reported that there were 120,000 fountains in the nation, which during that unprecedented year had done over a billion and a quarter dollars in business. As we already know, the fountain's days of glory were limited and they exist today only in small numbers. The nation did not lose just the fountain but also an American craftsman and folk hero of considerable proportion.

LAMENT FOR THE SODA JERK

Called soda clerk, dispenser, "the Professor," or soda jerk (after the practice of jerking the draft arm on the fountain), he, and occasionally she, rose and fell with the fortunes of the fountain itself. For years his stature was akin to that reserved today for the rock musician, and young men often worked months— even years—in the syrup room or as a dishwasher or broom pusher to get their chance behind the counter. Except for small out-of-the-way fountains, they worked in pairs and shared a multitude of roles—innovator, linguist, entertainer, stylist, neighborhood counselor, and, above all, concocter. They ranged in age from teenagers to the elderly, and for a long time it was as much a calling and profession as that of the druggists they often worked for. During the 1920s and into the 1930s when the great, fashionable urban streets boasted scores of fountains and ice cream parlors, there was the dream of mobility as the small-town soda jerk waited to be discovered and then installed as the new phenomenon of Broadway, Harvard Square, or downtown St. Louis. He became as much a particularly American figure as the cowboy or the lumberjack and was honored in song, poem, short story, joke, and film. His epic was a film serial of 1932 called *Fighting Blood,* starring George O'Hare as a tender but tough soda jerk who defends the honor of the innocent, becomes a champion prizefighter, and goes on to make a fortune with a drink he invents at his fountain.

The soda dispenser was not without technical advice: the first forty years of this century saw dozens of manuals and formularies created to pass along the hundreds of recipes required to be known by the professional. Aside from formulas, these handbooks gave tips on developing style and grace as a dispenser and told of the rewards waiting at the top of the profession. Said E. F. White in his *Spatula Soda Water Guide* of 1919: "Dispensing soda water as it exists today is an art and really good dispensers, either men or women, are scarce. Those at the top command good salaries. . . . [However,] true excellence takes years of practice." The best could not only expect financial reward but a certain degree of fame. Men like Ralph Hersch, chief soda clerk at the Waldorf Astoria during the 1920s and soda jerk to such notables as Sir Thomas Lipton and the young Prince of Wales, and C. L. Taylor, a jerker who had risen from the ranks to become the nation's ranking expert on chocolate concoctions, enjoyed nationwide reputations for their skills. Others who did not get written up in the mainstream media were honored in "Who's Who in the Soda Fountain World," a regular feature of *Soda Fountain* magazine. Typical of the entries in that section was this one for a highly seeded Pennsylvania soda jerk, which began:

Not so many years ago a young newsboy wandered up and down the streets of Chambersburg, Pennsylvania,

The king of the fountain was the soda jerk. This unidentified young man, caught in the act of fountain derring-do, practiced in Corpus Christi, Texas, in 1939 and was probably drafted into World War II, along with the manufacturers of soda fountain equipment, who were soon making airplane parts, rafts, detachable gasoline tanks and the like.

and every time he passed a soda fountain he looked longingly through the window and dreamed of the day he would become a soda man. Thirteen years ago that dream came true, and since then Donald Haller has made a real place for himself in the soda fountain world.

Though gone from the scene today, much of the art and science of the soda jerk has been saved through the aforementioned handbooks and trade magazines published during their reign. (A sampling of these appears in the last chapter of this book, where many of the techniques and formulas are revealed.) It is also fortunate that a few scholars paid attention to the soda jerk before his demise and recorded for all time what was to many the sodaman's most fascinating and disarming ability.

THUS HE SPOKE

As has been true of other trades and crafts, soda jerking produced its own jargon. In this case it was a particularly distinct and rich manner of speaking, which was the result of a variety of factors. It had functional uses. It was a system whereby a deadbeat leaving without paying his bill could be quickly and unobtrusively identified with the call, "Ninety-five." The fact that the boss was on his way could be signaled with the term "White Bread" or the number "Ninety-eight," and the feelings of a customer could be spared as "Mary Garden" or "M.G. Cocktail" was passed on as an order for citrate of magnesia. Complex orders could be telescoped into quick calls, and the bizarre terms themselves served as memory aids. Perhaps the most important factor was that it gave the soda jerk an identity and a chance to show off for an audience. The jerker was usually a young but special person who, like the railroad man or hobo, saw his as a calling requiring an argot of its own. Unlike other jargons, however, it was meant for showing off, and for that reason there was a host of terms for almost everything. For example, an order for a cup of black coffee became such calls as, "Mug of murk," "Draw one," "Leg off a pair of drawers," "In the dark," "Midnight," and "No cow."

Scholars are at a loss to pinpoint the time when the language began to take shape, but there is evidence that it was in the nineteenth century. For instance, it is known that preacher/orator Henry Ward Beecher (1813–1887) was intrigued by it and never missed a chance to test its dexterity. Beecher often told of going into a fountain and ordering two fried eggs on toast which was relayed as the classic call, "Adam and Eve on a raft." Beecher then puckishly asked that the eggs be scrambled and without hesitation the counterman added, "And wreck 'em."

The vitality and universality of the tongue more or less followed the course of the fountain itself, appearing at its strongest from the beginning of the century through the mid-1930s. The ability to speak this national tongue—once as important a criterion for a fountain job as knowing the difference between the Tulip Sundae Dish and the Crimped Parfait—is practically nonexistent today. Its long and agonizing death began in the late 1930s when Columbia University linguistics specialist W. Bentley observed, "The craze for this sort of fountain entertainment seems to be on the wane. Indeed the practice is frowned upon in many fountains, particularly those owned or operated by large chain organizations or department stores." It was a smart, cocky

REVOLVING TUMBLER WASHER.

THIS new and beautiful device does its work thoroughly as a washer, and at the same time its activity gives a pleasing variety to the counter arrangements. The tumblers rest on a platform revolving on a centre pivot. A jet of water washes the inside of each glass as it passes under the vase, the outside being cleansed by the waste from the water-jet above. A very slight force of water is sufficient to run it. *It is the best washer in the market.*

Space occupied on the counter 20 x 20 inches.

Height with water-jet 36 inches.	Price . . $90.00
" " bouquet-holder 24 inches.	Price . . 75 00

The New-York Historical Society
As such fountain giants as John Matthews, A. D. Puffer, Charles Lippincott and C. D. Dows fought for the lion's share of the market, ornateness became a great selling point, as shown by this offering from the Chas. Lippincott and Co. catalog of 1883.

tongue which at its most outlandish included calls like "Belly-wash," "Maggot," "Dog," and "Graveyard stew"—terms that apparently did not sit well with the policymakers employed by emerging giants of the Whelan/Walgreen ilk.

Luckily Bentley and several others paid attention to the now moribund tongue and recorded it. Two works are especially important: Bentley's "Linguistic Concoctions of the Soda Jerker" (*American Speech,* Vol. II, No. 1, February, 1936) and Michael Owen Jones's "Soda-Fountain, Restaurant and Tavern Calls" (*American Speech,* Vol. XLII, No. 1, February, 1967). Bentley's ambitious work was based on a year's observation in New York soda fountains, while Jones's compilation emerged from interviews with Paul Sinclair who was associated with the Jayhawk Café in Lawrence, Kansas, from the late 1930s to the mid-1960s. The old calls had held on at the Jayhawk long after they died elsewhere and Sinclair was able to recall them for Jones.

Based primarily on these two works and leaning some on others, such as H. L. Mencken's *The American Language, Supplement II* and John Lancaster Riordan's "Soda Fountain Lingo" (*California Folklore Quarterly,* Vol. IV [1945], 50–57), an abbreviated list of calls is assembled here. The presentation is made both to display the vitality of that lost tongue and to offer a guide to those wishing to revive it.

ADAM'S ALE   Water
ALL THE WAY   Used when ordering chocolate (or fudge) cake with chocolate ice cream
AND ANOTHER   Coffee
A-PIE   Apple pie

BABY   Glass of milk

BARKED PIE   Pie with upper crust

BELCH WATER   Glass of seltzer

BLACK AND WHITE   Chocolate soda with vanilla ice cream or chocolate malted milk (*Obs.*)

BLACK BOTTOM   Chocolate sundae with chocolate topping

BLACK STICK   Chocolate ice cream cone

BLUE-BOTTLE   Bromo

BOTTOM   Ice cream in a drink

BREAK IT AND SHAKE IT   Put eggs in a drink or whatever

BRIDGE   Four of anything (sometimes stated, A bridge party)

BUCKET OF . . .   A large scoop

BUCKET OF HAIL   Small glass of ice

BURN   A malted milk shake, chocolate unless otherwise specified

BURN IT AND LET IT SWIM   Float

BURN ONE ALL THE WAY   Chocolate malted with chocolate ice cream

CANARY ISLAND SPECIAL   Vanilla soda with chocolate ice cream

CAT'S EYES   Tapioca

CHASE   Pass (verb)

CHICAGO   Pineapple soda, but sometimes pineapple sundae

CHOC IN   Chocolate soda

CITY JUICE   Water

CLEAN UP THE KITCHEN   Hamburger or hash

C.O. HIGHBALL   Castor oil

COFF   Coffee or coffee ice cream

COKE PIE   Coconut pie

COLD SPOT   Glass of iced tea

CONEY ISLAND CHICKEN   Frankfurter

COW JUICE   Milk

C-PIE   Cherry pie

CROWD   Three of anything (believed to have derived from "Two's company and three's a crowd")

DOG AND MAGGOT   Cracker and cheese

DOG or DOG BISCUIT   Cracker

DOG SOUP   Water

DRAW ONE   Cup of coffee

DROP   A sundae

DUSTY MILLER   Chocolate sundae with malted milk

ECHO   Repeat the order

EIGHTY-ONE   Glass of water

EIGHTY-SEVEN AND A HALF   Attractive female approaching

EIGHTY-SIX   We don't have or are out of the item ordered. (Jones suggests that this term was taken from railroad jargon, where it was used in telegraphy to say that a yard was unable to fill an order.)

EIGHTY-TWO   Two glasses of water

FIFTY-FIVE   Root beer

FIFTY-ONE   Hot chocolate

FILET   À la mode

FIRST LADY   Spare ribs

FIVE   Large glass of milk

FIX THE PUMPS   A customer with large breasts

FIZZ   Carbonated water

FLY CAKE   Raisin cake

FORTY-ONE   Lemonade

FOURTEEN   A special order, listen carefully

FREEZE ONE   Chocolate frosted

GENTLEMAN WILL TAKE A CHANCE   Hash

GEORGE EDDY   Customer who leaves no tip

GLOB   Plain sundae

GO FOR A WALK   To take out

GORP   Greedy eater

GRAVEYARD STEW   Milk toast

GROUND HOG   Hot dog

H_2O Water

HANDFUL   Five (Handful plus one, A pair, Crowd, etc.,
   used for six, seven, and so forth)

HEMORRHAGE   Ketchup

HIGH YELLOW BLACK AND WHITE   Chocolate soda with vanilla
   ice cream

HOBOKEN SPECIAL   Pineapple soda with chocolate ice cream

HOLD THE HAIL   No ice

HOPS   Malted milk extract

HOT CHA   Hot chocolate (also, Hot cup and Hot top)

HOT SPOT   Tea

HOUSE BOAT   Banana split

ICE THE RICE   Rice pudding with ice cream

IN   Soda

IN THE AIR   A large glass

IN THE HAY   Strawberry milk shake

INHALE   To drink

JAVA   Coffee

JERK   An ice cream soda (This term derives from the jerking of the fountain lever forward to make the carbonated
   water spray.)

L.A.   À la mode

LOAD OF   Plate of anything

LONG COKE   Large Coke

LOOSENERS   Prunes

L-PIE   Lemon pie

LUMBER   Toothpick

M.D.   Dr. Pepper

M.G.   Dose of citrate of magnesia

MAIDEN'S DELIGHT   Cherries

MAKE IT VIRTUE   Cherry Coke

MARY GARDEN   Dose of citrate of magnesia

MODE MODE   Two scoops of ice cream with pie or cake

MOISTURE   Water

MUD   Chocolate ice cream

MYSTERY   Chocolate and vanilla sundae

NATURAL   7-Up (from the combination of 5 and 2, which is a
    natural in craps)

NERVOUS PUDDING   Jell-O

NINETY-EIGHT   The manager; sometimes, the assistant soda
    man

NINETY-FIVE   Called when a customer is walking out with-
    out paying

NINETY-NINE   Head soda man

No cow   Without milk

OH GEE   Orangeade

O.J.   Orange juice

ON   All sundaes

ON WHEELS   To go

ONE IN ALL THE WAY   Chocolate soda with chocolate ice
    cream

ONE ON THE CITY   Water

ONE ON THE COUNTRY   Buttermilk

PAIR   Two

PAIR OF DRAWERS   Two cups of coffee

PATCH   Strawberry ice cream

PEST   Assistant manager

PINK STICK   Strawberry ice cream cone

PITTSBURGH   Toast, or something, is burning

POP BOY   Soda jerk who doesn't know his business

RHINELANDER   Chocolate soda with vanilla ice cream

RIFFLE   Refill the order

SALT WATER MAN   Ice cream mixer

SAND   Sugar

SCANDAL SOUP   Tea

SCOOP   Spoon

SHAKE ONE   Milk shake, chocolate unless otherwise specified

SHOOT IT YELLOW   Lemon Coke

SHOOT ONE   Coke

SHOOT ONE FROM THE SOUTH   Especially strong Coke

SHOT   Small (6-ounce) Coke

SINKERS AND SUDS   Coffee and doughnuts

SODA CLERK   Soda man in top-rated fountain

SPLA   Whipped cream

SPLIT ONE   Banana split

SQUEEZE ONE   Orange juice

SQUIRT   Soda dispenser

STRETCH ONE   Large Coke

SUDS   Root Beer

THIRTEEN   One of the big bosses is around

THIRTY-ONE   Lemonade

THROUGH GEORGIA   Chocolate syrup added

To the left   Lemon flavor, which traditionally appeared
   to the left of the Coke syrup pump

To the right   Cherry flavor, which was dispensed from the
   right of the Coke

Tools   Table utensils

Twenty-one   Limeade

Twist it, choke it, and make it cackle   Chocolate malted
   with egg

Van   Vanilla ice cream

Vanilla   There's a pretty girl out in front

Virgin Coke   Coke with cherry

Western   Coke with chocolate flavor

White cow   Vanilla milk shake

White one   Small (6-ounce) milk

White stick   Vanilla cone

Yum-yum   Sugar

Armed with this admittedly small sampling of the total vo-
cabulary, the challenge is putting the terms into the full rhythmic
calls of the soda jerk. With a little practice, three strawberry
milk shakes become ''Shake a crowd of patch,'' while three large
glasses of ice are, ''Hail a crowd in the air,'' and four chocolate
sodas translate to ''Jerk a bridge through Georgia.''

VII

The Anatomy of Ice Cream

ALTHOUGH THE precise food value of ice cream depends on the value of its component parts, generally speaking it is a nutritious and caloric frozen dessert which the federal government officially classifies as a "food." On the average it has more fat (3 to 4 times more) and more calcium (about 15 percent more) than plain milk. Though rich in calories as a "food," it is relatively low in calories as a "dessert"; for example, a half-cup of ice cream is about equal in calories to a plain cookie three inches in diameter.

ICE CREAM TODAY

Generally speaking, ice cream is a blend of dairy products, sugar, flavoring, sometimes eggs, federally approved additives, and air. The latter ''ingredient'' may come as a surprise to some, but without it ice cream would be an icy lump rather than ice *cream*. Needless to say, there are limits: too much air yields a snowy, fluffy, ''dry,'' dull ice cream, while too little yields a heavy, soggy mass which experts say resists flavoring. However, today's consumer need not worry about getting too little air. Within this basic framework of ingredients there is a broad range of alternative possibilities from fresh-from-the-farm flavors to synthetic ones, from sweet cream to powdered milk, and from vegetable to chemical additives.

There are almost as many commercial ice cream formulas as there are brands of ice cream. As a result any of the following may be present: sweet cream, frozen cream, plastic cream (not what it sounds like, it is actually a very rich dairy cream), whole milk, skim milk, buttermilk, butter, butter oil, nonfat dry milk, several varieties of condensed milk, evaporated milk, powdered whey solids, malted milk, cane sugar, beet sugar, sucrose, brown sugar, honey, corn sweeteners, corn syrup, corn-syrup solids, dextrose, maltose syrup, fructose, fresh eggs, frozen eggs, powdered eggs, salt, colorings, a wide variety of natural and man-made flavorings, and a long list of items known as emulsifiers and stabilizers.

The last two terms require some explanation. Stabilizers and emulsifiers are extras added to most commercial ice creams in very small quantities. Stabilizers are used to prevent ice crystals from forming in the ice cream and are of two general types: gelatins, from animal sources, and vegetables ranging from Irish moss to oat gum. Emulsifiers are a relatively new class of additives which are added to smooth, fill, and render ice cream more whippable. Most of them derive from either natural glycerides or hexahydric alcohols, glycol, and glycol ester. Alabama prohibits their use and several other states impose stricter limits on their use than federal standards permit. Although few commercial ice creams do not have both stabilizers and emulsifiers, ice cream expert Dr. Wendell Arbuckle pointed out in his textbook *Ice Cream:* "Excellent ice cream can be made and considerable amounts are made without the use of a stabilizer or an emulsifier. Since milk and milk products contain natural stabilizing and emulsifying materials . . . mixes of certain composition and processing treatment may be stabilized by the effect of these natural materials." Emulsifiers have been a matter of some controversy and not just among natural food devotees. *Consumer Bulletin* reported in 1962 that certain ice cream emulsifiers and their chemical relatives approved by the Food and Drug Administration had produced severe illnesses in laboratory animals when administered in large doses.

The difference between ice creams is directly tied to the quality, richness, and freshness of all of the aforementioned ingredients and the way they are blended and cared for. An "economy" ice cream will rely more heavily on dried products, air, a low percentage of milk fats (10 to 12 percent) and will normally contain the maximum amount of stabilizers and emulsifiers. A high quality ice cream will rely on fresh whole products, be less airy, contain 16 to 20 percent milk fat and employ additives sparingly. To the connoisseur these differences are dramatic. "Ice cream is like wine," said Gael Greene in *New York* magazine. "It ranges from the meanest *vin ordinaire* to the *grand cru* yield of the great châteaus." The analogy is perfect; however, the ice cream lover is at a monumental disadvantage over his or her cork-sniffing counterpart in that there is no detailed label or

111

classification system to help in selecting the "right ice cream." As Dr. Arbuckle says in *Ice Cream:* "Market grades or classes have not as yet been accepted in the ice cream industry in spite of the fact that many consumers would welcome a system of market grades."

JUST AND UNJUST DESSERTS

Not only is ice cream exempted from laws that require ingredient labeling, but those things that do appear on the carton are not very helpful and are occasionally deceptive. Investigative reporter Coleman McCarthy of the Washington *Post* wrote of going to an ice cream plant and asking to see where the company's top-of-the-line "hand packed" ice cream was packed (McCarthy, like all ice cream buffs, knows that hand packed is the best). McCarthy found that the "hand packed" ice cream was hand-held under the filling machine on the assembly line like most regular ice creams. Confronted with this, a company official told McCarthy, "We say 'hand packed' not 'hand dipped.' That's pretty clever, isn't it?"

The help that we do get is the federal provision that requires artificial flavors to be so noted with terms like "vanilla flavored" and "artificial vanilla added." Also, by federal law, only ice cream with eggs in it can be called "French." Although as far back as 1914 there was a movement afoot in the nation's newspapers to get ingredients listed on ice cream cartons, the organized industry has batted down every labeling proposal since then (including that of adding ice cream to the recent Fair Packaging and Labeling Act) and is still actively doing so. In the July,

1971, issue of *Up to Date,* the newsletter of the Milk Industry Foundation and the International Association of Ice Cream Manufacturers, it was reported that the two groups were working against a group of Washington law students (calling themselves "Label Inc.") who were trying to get the government to insist on lists of ingredients on *all* products. Said the newsletter:

> For a number of sound reasons, such labeling is totally inappropriate for many dairy products. It's an impossible requirement for ice cream as an example, because of the many, many optional ingredients available. Moreover labeling names of some ingredients and the amounts would likely be misleading in many ways to consumers.

Second only to the long-waged war against ingredient labeling is that against sale by weight, which has also been waged for many years. The sale of ice cream by volume, of course, predominates. Federal standards require that ice cream weigh at least 4.5 pounds a gallon or it is not ice cream; however, this minimum grants considerable latitude. While homemade ice cream or truly deluxe commercial brands will weigh in at close to twice the minimum, most low-grade supermarket brands come so close to the 4.5 pound minimum that if one of these weighs in higher it is probably an indictment of your scale rather than cause for thanking the manufacturer. Today's commercial ice creams range from a robust 20 to 40 percent air to an anemic 50 percent or more, but ice cream manufacturers do not like to talk about such things as air and weight, and only a few will divulge their air percentages.

This obfuscation of the content and condition of ice cream

82d CONGRESS
1st SESSION

H. R. 3517

IN THE HOUSE OF REPRESENTATIVES

APRIL 4, 1951

Mr. FALLON introduced the following bill; which was referred to the Committee on the Judiciary

---

A BILL

Designating June 15, 1951, as National Ice Cream Day.

1   *Be it enacted by the Senate and House of Representa-*

2 *tives of the United States of America in Congress assembled,*

3 That June 15, 1951, is hereby designated as National Ice

4 Cream Day.

5   The President is authorized to issue a proclamation call-

6 ing upon officials of the Government and inviting the

7 people of the United States to observe such a day with

8 appropriate ceremonies.

9   The President is also requested to communicate this

10 declaration, by proclamation or otherwise, to the governors

11 of the several States, and request them to take such action

12 as they may deem advisable in order to bring about ob-

13 servance of such day.

Maryland Historical Society
One of several bills proposed to take official recognition of the fact that the ice cream industry was about to be 100 years old. Despite hard plumping by the Pooh-Bahs of the ice cream industry, an effort to have ice cream featured on the face of a 1951 commemorative postage stamp failed.

is not just the handiwork of the industry and its powerful Washington lobby, but has government as an accomplice. Ice cream, along with a few other privileged products such as soft drinks, is exempted from ingredient labeling and other nuisances because the government has granted it what is termed "a standard of identity." This means that if a product meets those standards, it is ice cream, whether it is a superior blend of fresh ingredients or an inferior airy substance hardly worthy of the name—that is, hardly worthy of the name outside the corridors of the Food and Drug Administration. These standards were established after *twenty-four years* of give and take between government and industry, which provided lots of time for give on the part of the government, as the 38,000-page hearing record shows. As it is put quite candidly by Robert North, who heads the International Association of Ice Cream Manufacturers, "Our organization really got started fighting federal standards and now we fight to maintain them."

Besides saying that ice cream must weigh 4.5 pounds per gallon, the government says it must contain 10 percent butterfat, and goes on to permit a broad variety of ingredients including small amounts of chemical dyes, stabilizers, and emulsifiers. One of the main reasons that the industry balks at labeling is that it fears consumer reaction to the names of these federally approved additives. But the industry's concern for our sensibilities is little solace to the ice cream consumer looking for blends of fresh cream, cane sugar, and eggs rather than tetrasodium pyrophosphate, dried cheese whey, polysorbate 80, propylene glycol, seaweed derivatives, dried corn syrup, and the like. In short, we have no way of knowing who has taken the advice of the American Food Laboratories, whose ads in *Dairy and Ice Cream Field* magazine read: "Imitation Products, Real Profits."

This lack of frankness and bewildering array of additives is beginning to attract some deserving attention. *Consumer Bulletin* says, "The proverbial purchaser of a pig in a poke had nothing on the buyer of ice cream in our modern age of palatial supermarkets." The influential Gael Greene was moved to conclude, "Most ice cream sold today is sadly 'mock.'" Observed Dow Jones's *National Observer* in reviewing supermarket ice creams, ". . . it comes as close to being completely synthetic as it legally can." Within the industry *Ice Cream World* has been pushing for an overall upgrading of ice cream (even though that might spell the end of the 69-cent half gallon) and a few manufacturers have begun to brag about their dedication to "natural" and "fresh" ingredients—a trend which has others in the ice cream industry (not to mention the chemical industry) upset. Perhaps most telling were the remarks delivered in 1969 by Mrs. Virginia Knauer, Special Assistant to President Nixon for Consumer Affairs, to a group of ice cream manufacturers. She said, in part: "But to say that the consumer is confused is putting it mildly. If there's a Federal standard for it, he can't even be sure of the exact ingredients. . . . Perhaps we in the Federal government should take a new look at our entire food standards requirements." She added: "I . . . believe the consumer should be better informed on the use of food additives. The average person eats about 3½ pounds of assorted additives a year. The use of chemical food additives—for flavor, for color, and for other purposes—has increased 50 percent in the last few years, so that we now have nearly 3,000 additives on the market. How many more will we have five or 10 years from now? What are we going to add to the additives?" The industry reacted negatively to the Knauer remarks. (Carped *Dairy and Ice Cream Field:* "As far as the dairy industry is concerned, one thing remains clearly evident—housewives, including Mrs. Knauer, need more education about how ice cream is made and what it costs. . . .") Since the speech nothing has changed and the consumer is still "protected" from nasty-sounding ingredients. What is puzzling about all this is the remarkable lack of information the industry gives out. Who knows, maybe seaweed and locust-gum is better for us than traditional ingredients, but the industry is conspicuously silent when it comes to making its case for them or letting us know that we are eating them.

Yet amid all this there are many superior ice creams on the market today—ice cream as good as has ever been served—and indications are that their number is increasing.

How then do we know which are these superior brands? The only real way is to taste them and subjectively judge, just as the wine taster must ultimately do (despite labels, in the final analysis, of course, it is the wine and not the florid label that we taste). The combination of fresh ingredients, low to moderate overrun, real robust flavoring agents, high percentage of butterfat, and avoidance of such indiscretions as "heat shock" (that careless treatment of ice cream which causes globs of ice to form in reaction to jarring differences in temperature) will almost always win out. Though imperfect, price is another useful guide. Needless to say, there are some inferior ice creams overpriced and some excellent ones (often found in rural areas) which are pleasantly inexpensive. Generally, however, you pay more for such brands as Louis Sherry, Baskin-Robbins, Swensen's, Häagen-Dazs, Petersen's, Friendly's, Schrafft's, Howard Johnson's, and the like because they range from very good to great.

Howard Johnson's

The first of 1200 Howard Johnson's opened in 1925 in this store in Wollaston, Massachusetts. From the outset Howard Deering Johnson's big product was ice cream, which he made in the basement in a secondhand freezer. He later worked out a deal with a local businessman who agreed to pay a fee for the Johnson name and the right to buy supplies from him—giving Johnson claim to the title of father of American franchisers.

Mrs. Anita Stickney, who heads the small northeastern chain of Deering Ice Cream Shops (which, for what it is worth, sells an ice cream that the author and his wife contend is the best they have ever tasted), says that there are many criteria for judging ice cream, but none is more important than the use of *fresh* ingredients, blended without scrimping and sped to the mouth of the consumer with care. She adds, "About the best way to tell if fresh ingredients are in the ice cream is to taste it. If an ice cream has a lot of stabilizer, for example, it simply won't taste fresh and good." What bothers Mrs. Stickney and others who produce high quality ice cream is that much of the good ice cream is being bought by adults for themselves and their guests while a half gallon of *ersatz* ice cream is brought home for the kids. As she puts it, "I'd hate to see the day when young people can't tell the difference because they've never tasted good ice cream."

It is perhaps too much to hope for, but the revival of interest in good ice cream may help upgrade the general level and tone of American ice cream to its highest level ever. Meanwhile we can be thankful that there are superior ice creams, that there are at least some federal standards (for a long while there were none), and that the average bowl of new-fashioned ice cream is much cleaner than its old-fashioned counterpart.

To their credit, the ice cream industry and government have worked continually to improve and maintain the sanitary conditions that surround ice cream, thus relegating the ice cream–caused epidemic and individual illness to things of the past. In fact, according to a Cornell University study of a few years ago, if a person with average luck were to eat ice cream every day it would take him or her 100,000,000 years to come down with an upset stomach. Lest we forget, there was a time when ice cream lovers paid dearly for their passion. Starting with an outbreak of vanilla ice cream poisoning in Norway in 1848, up through an ice cream–caused paratyphoid epidemic in England during 1946, there have been over one hundred official government reports on public health problems caused by ice cream. A particularly chilling article in the *American Journal of Public Health* of September, 1926, gave the grim details on some of the by-products of old-fashioned American ice cream, including a Rhode Island diphtheria epidemic of 417 cases and an Alabama typhoid outbreak affecting 350 people. As late as 1935 F. J. Schlink, co-author of the muckraking classic *100,000,000 Guinea Pigs,* observed in his book *Eat, Drink and Be Wary* that public health regulations regarding ice cream lagged far behind those for milk and then went on to recite a series of bacterial horror stories.*

From the consumer's standpoint, ice cream technology has brought a mixed lot of steps backward, like all the aforementioned chemical shortcuts, and quantum leaps forward, such as the vast improvement of sanitary conditions brought about by new equipment, research, tests, and so forth. A far less critical, but no less interesting, advance that can be seen and consumed is the result of the dedicated effort on the part of a handful of professionals who have dramatically widened the horizons of ice cream flavoring.

THE ARTFUL TECHNICIANS OF FLAVOR

Each spring the trade magazine *Dairy and Ice Cream Field* unveils its annual ''Survey of Frozen Dessert Trends,'' and each

---

* Considering all this, it is a wonder that so many of today's manufacturers advertise their ice cream as ''old-fashioned.''

spring under the heading "Sales by Flavor" those three pillars, vanilla, chocolate, and strawberry, appear in just that order. In its spring, 1971, survey it was reported that in the previous year vanilla had accounted for 51 percent of all ice cream sold, which means that everything else, including chocolate (13.5 percent) and strawberry (6 percent), had to be considered an "also-ran." Butter pecan accounted for only 2.4 percent and coffee came in at a surprisingly low 1 percent.* At the bottom of the list of traditional flavors was a category called "other" which had jumped from 2.7 percent of the market in 1969 to 5.7 percent in 1970. As any child knows, hidden behind this bland-sounding "other" lurks ice-creamdom's most exciting front, a place where vanilla ice cream is a component rather than an end product.

The ability to take flavor is one of the most remarkable facets of ice cream. The nation's basic flavors were originally developed to use local commodities in abundant supply and to cater to local taste. As a result, not too many years ago blueberry ice cream was an almost totally regional delicacy. Even today when there is much talk of an increasingly homogenized American palate, regional preferences are still strong when it comes to ice cream—although not nearly as strong as they once were. Coffee does much better in the northeast than elsewhere, but time was when it was all but a New England exclusive. Today, however, ginger, grapenut, and frozen pudding are rare outside New England, where they are popular. Maple flavors are very popular in Canada, and Californians go for such flavors as date and prune, which have never made it big nationally. Peanut and candy flavors generally bomb in New York but do well in the

---

* Just as vanilla walks away in the ice cream list, orange dominates (40 percent) among sherbets with pineapple, lime, lemon, raspberry, and "other" following in that order.

south. Texans will buy anything with pecans in it but still balk at such alien notions as blueberry. What's more, even seemingly standard flavors are subject to regional proclivities. It is all but impossible to sell a quality vanilla to a knowing Philadelphian without those little black specks of the vanilla bean displayed conspicuously against a very white field; yet, elsewhere yellow vanilla is preferred and people complain about the flecks. New Yorkers generally like their coffee ice cream strong, while Bostonians go for a milder blend.

Meanwhile the number of flavors is increasing at an unbelievable rate. Robert North of the International Association of Ice Cream Manufacturers comments on this growth: "We once kept a flavor 'log' but quit when it hit 247. Today it's well over four hundred, but it is almost impossible to catalog them and keep them straight. For example, what do you do with something called 'shortberry strawcake'?" North adds that the total would jump far beyond four hundred if you counted all of the products of what he calls "wildcatting at the dairy schools"—reference to a trend to fearless flavor experimentation which has cropped up in recent years at such dairy-strong agricultural schools as those at Penn State, Ohio State, the University of Wisconsin, and the University of Maryland.

Wildcatting is the product of several factors. Flavor science has advanced rapidly and it is the wont of professors and students to flex that technology. Intercollegiate competition is at play with a certain prestige involved as one comes up with the first great watercress sherbet. Finally there is the factor of helping to develop new applications for local produce in long supply; for instance, the University of Maryland invented sweet potato ice cream to help that state's farmers. The University of

Wisconsin, for example, is responsible for such innovations as buttermint toffee, banana marshmallow, apple strudel, and pumpkin-pie marble. Citrus ice creams (not sherbets) were developed at the University of Florida.

By far the most flamboyant flavors come from the Ohio State University Department of Dairy Technology, which has perfected sauerkraut sherbet and such ice creams as potatoes and bacon, brassicaceous beer (horseradish and root beer), squash, and mustard. Such imaginative and sometimes nauseating flavors are not only the product of the university lab; private industry has come up with bubble gum, sunflower seed, pumpkin-licorice, and jelly bean. Perhaps the all-time biggest bomb—for obvious reasons—was the Chili Con Carne Good Humor.

One of the leading centers for flavor is the Department of Dairy Science at the University of Maryland, where matters concerning ice cream center around Dr. Wendell S. Arbuckle, professor and one of the nation's leading experts in the field of frozen desserts. Arbuckle has long been involved in creating new flavors on demand. For example, a request from a Boston manufacturer for mint-tea ice cream yielded a product now on sale in Massachusetts, and he developed the aforementioned sweet potato for the Maryland Sweet Potato Growers' Association, who were looking for a new outlet for their product. Recently, in the role of consultant, he worked with an almond growers' association to develop twenty-odd almond specialties such as brandied apricot almond and banana almond. Though a flavor expert of the first order, Arbuckle looks upon this specialty as a sidelight to his more fundamental efforts in basic research and new types of ice creams. He has researched and written extensively on the chemical and physical properties of ice cream and his highly technical book *Ice Cream* is the dominant textbook and how-to manual for the industry. The application of his fundamental knowledge has led to a variety of innovations. Arbuckle invented Parevine, a kosher ice cream which leaves out milk, meat, and their derivatives in favor of eggs and edible oils. Parevine has passed standards and is now sold in five northeastern states. He did much of the work on diabetic ice creams now available in many locations and has worked along with the Department of Agriculture in using ghee—a buffalo milk product—as a substitute for butterfat in ice cream.

Outside the university, the top flavor innovators are located in the flavor-supply houses and the flavor-oriented ice cream companies. A good example of the latter is Baskin-Robbins, where a basic element in that company's plan for world conquest is its arsenal of flavors; for that reason hundreds of new concoctions are created in its Burbank laboratories each year. Only a small percentage makes it past the company's test panel and its veto-carrying president, Irv Robbins, to market as Baskin-Robbins originals. Some of the lab's most famous creations are tanganilla (a tangerine-vanilla marriage), banana daiquiri, mandarin chocolate sherbet, espresso, mince pie, boysenberry cheesecake, German chocolate cake, pistachio almond fudge, caramel coconut, pink grapefruit ice, English toffee, and that ever-popular sensation jamoca almond fudge. One of the major sources of inspiration is customer suggestions, which roll in by the score. For example, one customer told the late Burt Baskin that the people who think up flavors must be "plumb nuts," which was all that was needed to inspire plum nuts (plums, vanilla, and walnuts).

As a consequence, the firm's capacity to flavor is not taken lightly. In February, 1967, during a rambling two-hour-and-fifteen-minute telecast, Cuban premier and known ice cream buff, Fidel Castro, boasted that his country would soon be able to produce more ice cream flavors than the United States. Castro added that the Cuban industry had achieved twenty-six flavors and would soon put the United States to shame with forty-two. When UPI flashed a report of this claim across the country, Irv Robbins himself immediately placed a call to Castro, who could not be reached. Robbins finally settled for Cuba's minister of information, who was informed that Baskin-Robbins alone possessed a repertoire of over 290 flavors. By the time of Baskin-Robbins's twenty-fifth anniversary in 1971 that total had climbed to 401, although it contained certain permanently retired items like goody-goody gumdrop, a 1965 flavor containing tiny, frozen, tooth-threatening gumdrops. The 401 total (recently boosted to 431) is authentic and was enough to get Baskin-Robbins listed in *Guinness' Book of Records* along with its claim to the largest ice cream sundae—a monster valued at $750, which was made with 600 pounds of ice cream, 34 quarts of sauce, and 153 ounces of nuts. (This latter record fell in 1971 when several Seattle citizens produced an 865-pound sundae.)

Although the pace of innovation is especially manic at Baskin-Robbins, other companies are deeply committed to the flavor race. Chicago's Bresler's Ice Cream Company, a strong Baskin-Robbins competitor with a lesser but still impressive flavor count of 201, first introduced such house specialties as iced tea, root beer, bubble gum, and bittersweet chocolate. And not to be overlooked is Good Humor, which year after year unveils imaginative spring models like jolly gingerbread, chocolate chip candy, Danish fruitcake, and watermelon ice.

Unlike other more esoteric technologies, flavor research and development can be performed in the sanctity of the home laboratory (often called the kitchen). To aid those interested in this delightful pursuit, a "flavor seminar" is forthcoming, but first you need to know how to make the basic raw material: vanilla ice cream.

VIII

Making It—A Basic Course in Ice Cream Construction

D o - i t - y o u r s e l f ice cream has both drawbacks and advantages. One drawback is that it takes time, effort, and requires undivided attention, especially when one is at the novice stage, just acquiring his or her cold thumb. Furthermore, homemade ice cream has a short shelf-life and begins to go slowly into a hard and icy decline after twenty-four hours because it lacks the preserving additives of commercial ice creams.

As for the advantages: your product—eaten fresh—will be generally superior to its average commercial counterpart. Technology being what it is, it is impossible to pump as much air into ice cream at home as it is in the factory, which virtually guarantees you a dense, rich blend generally twice as heavy as the kind you buy in the store. It is cheaper, can be customized to your individual taste, and offers unlimited opportunity to experiment with mixes and flavors—some say an end in itself. Finally, you do not have to compete commercially so you don't have to skimp on rich ingredients, infuse it with hocus-pocus stabilizers and emusifiers, or tone it up with colors from a chemical palette.

With the aid of such experts as Dr. Arbuckle and the Department of Agriculture Research Service, the essentials of home ice cream construction and experimentation are unveiled in this chapter. It is intended to serve as a handbook for the reader, giving all that is required to become a competent manufacturer, and will range in complexity from simple cranking instructions to some fairly esoteric skills, such as the secrets of flavoring persimmon and sweet potato ice creams.

CRANKING OUT A GOOD VANILLA

Even if vanilla is not your favorite flavor, it is imperative that you learn to make it first, for it is the basis for almost all other ice creams (essentially flavored vanillas). Put simply: if you cannot make a good vanilla, you will never make a great chocolate or a superior coffee.

The two basic elements you will need are an ice cream freezer (hand-crank or electric) and a mix.

Freezers come in several shapes and sizes, and the decision as to what model you need is your own.* The function of all freezers is to stir and aerate the mix as it is freezing, which results in an increase in the volume of the mix by about one-third,

---

* Information on obtaining home freezers and other ice cream ingredients and paraphernalia is contained in the appendix.

TINGLEY'S PATENT
HORIZONTAL

ICE-CREAM FREEZER

Is · recommended for FAMILIES, HOTELS, SALOONS, and WHOLESALE MANUF. 'TURERS

As the best Ice-Cream Freezer in the market.

It saves ICE,
    Saves TIME,
        Saves LABOR,

And produces the finest quality of Cream known to the Art.

Send for Descriptive Catalogue.

CHAS. G. BLATCHLEY, Manufacturer,
506 COMMERCE STREET,
Philadelphia, Pa.

The Bettmann Archive
Tingley's was one of many freezers on the market around 1880 when this ad appeared. While each manufacturer boasted of the vast superiority of his product, all were basically the same.

Farrell's Inc.
BELOW: This nostalgic scene serves as the service mark for the expanding Farrell's chain of old-fashioned ice cream parlors.

creating small ice crystals and tiny air bubbles in the process. The size of these bubbles and pieces of ice determines the texture of the ice cream and, unless one prefers coarse, gritty ice cream, the aim is to keep them as small as possible for the smoothest end product.

The components of any freezer are the cranking mechanism, a metal can in which the mix is agitated, the dasher (which is the paddle doing the agitation), and a tub, which surrounds the can to hold the ice and salt that freezes the ice cream. Since dairy products offer an ideal culture for bacteria, it is essential that all pieces be kept clean at all times.

The actual freezing process goes like this:

1. Scald and wash the can, also its cover and dasher, and let cool.

2. Pour the chilled mix into the can, filling it two-thirds full (more will overflow, less will not let it freeze and whip properly).

3. Place the can in the freezer tub, putting the dasher, cover, and cranking mechanism in their proper places.

4. Pack the tub with salt (preferably rock salt) and crushed ice, using approximately 1 pound of salt for each 6 to 8 pounds of ice. Pack first with a layer of ice, then cover with a thin layer of salt. Continue layering with salt and ice until the can is covered. Add a small amount of water—one cup for a small freezer, two for larger models—to hasten freezing. (The quicker the freezing the smoother the ice cream.)

5. Begin cranking. With a hand model begin cranking slowly, then faster as the freezing starts. The mixture is ready when the turning becomes hard, which usually takes fifteen minutes or longer of vigorous cranking. With electric freezers, plug in, then unplug when you can hear the motor begin to labor. In either

case, before the cream begins to freeze the ice must melt enough to cause water to flow from the drain hole in the side of the tub (never let drain hole get plugged with ice). During the cranking process it will be necessary to add more salt and ice to keep the can covered.

6. Remove the crank mechanism, cover, and dasher, and cover the frozen mixture with wax paper or foil. Replace cover and plug the hole in its top with a cork.

7. Freeze for 2 to 3 hours. This can be accomplished either by placing the can in the freezer compartment of your refrigerator (wrapped in a towel, newspaper, or other form of insulation) or by emptying out the tub, replacing the can, and repacking with salt and ice.

The most common problem associated with this process is unsatisfactory freezing, which yields a grainy, icy, or mushy ice cream. If this happens to you, chances are your problem is one of these: (1) the ice is not crushed fine enough—the ice should really be smashed small for a smooth product, (2) you are using too little salt, (3) your freezer tub leaks or is not draining through the hole provided, which prevents the efficient heat transfer required, or (4) your mix has too much sugar, which slows down freezing.

With this procedure established, your next step is the selection of a vanilla mix. There are scores of basic formulas, ranging from very rich "catering quality" and Philadelphia vanillas to low-calorie and diabetic vanillas. These recipes (each yielding a gallon) should give you a broad repertoire with which to experiment.

FRENCH VANILLA (RICH) ICE CREAM MIX
(*Adapted from a U.S. Department of Agriculture formula*)

8 *cups light cream*   4 *teaspoons vanilla*
6 *eggs, separated*   ½ *teaspoon salt*
2 *cups sugar*

Beat egg yolks until smooth; add half the sugar, and beat until the sugar is dissolved. Beat the whites to a stiff froth, and stir into the yolk and sugar mixture. Add the cream and the rest of the sugar, and cook in a double boiler for 15 minutes, or until it has thickened. Stir while it cooks. Add salt and vanilla, and chill before placing in freezer canister.

LOW-FAT VANILLA ICE MILK
(*Adapted from University of Illinois College of Agriculture formula*)

2 *cups sugar*   3 *eggs, beaten*
¼ *cup cornstarch*   ½ *cup water*
¼ *teaspoon salt*   1 *tablespoon unflavored*
2 *quarts skim milk* (*can be*   *gelatin*
   made from instant nonfat   1½ *tablespoons vanilla*
   dry milk)

Mix sugar, cornstarch, and salt in a heavy pan. Gradually add 1 quart of milk. Cook over low heat, stirring constantly, until mixture is thickened (about 15 minutes). Stir a little of the hot cornstarch mixture into the beaten eggs; then stir the eggs into the remaining cornstarch mixture. Cook over low heat, stirring constantly, for 4 to 5 minutes. Soften gelatin in ½ cup of water for 5 minutes. Stir into hot mixture. Chill. Stir in vanilla and remaining quart of milk before freezing.

PHILADELPHIA VANILLA ICE CREAM
(Adapted from the formula used by Bassett's of Philadelphia)

3 *quarts light cream*	3 *vanilla beans (or 3*
3 *cups sugar*	*teaspoons vanilla*
	extract)

Combine 1 quart of cream, sugar, and split vanilla beans in top of double boiler over boiling water. Stir until cream is scalded (about 10 minutes). Remove from heat, scrape seeds and pulp from vanilla beans, discarding pods and returning seeds and pulp to the cream. Cool. (If extract is used, add after cream is removed from the heat.) Then add remaining cream and chill before using.

VANILLA CUSTARD ICE CREAM
VERY RICH CATERING QUALITY
(From The Ice Cream Cookbook *by Earl Goodman)*

1 *quart whipping cream*	4 *tablespoons vanilla*
1 *quart plus 3 cups whole milk*	3 *cups sugar*
12 *egg yolks*	2 *tablespoons salt*

Scald milk and cream in a 6-quart saucepan. In a large bowl, beat together yolks and salt. Slowly add about 3 cups of the hot milk to the egg yolks, stirring constantly. Then return this mixture to the milk in the pan. Add sugar and keep stirring while cooking at medium heat. When mixture coats spoon or just starts to boil, remove from heat. Add vanilla. In most cases the mix will be lumpy; strain out the lumps when you pour the mix into the freezer canister.

PLAIN VANILLA ICE CREAM

A GOOD WORKHORSE VANILLA WITHOUT EGGS

(From W. S. Arbuckle, University of Maryland)

1¾ *quarts light cream*	1 *tablespoon gelatin dissolved*
½ *pint evaporated milk*	*in ½ cup cold water*
1½ *cups sugar*	*Pinch of salt*
	1 *tablespoon vanilla*

This mix does not have to be cooked but the results will be more desirable if the ingredients are mixed and cooked in a double boiler at a temperature of 145° to 150° and then cooled.

With such basic formulas as a guide, one may wish to experiment with other vanillas. These general principles are worth keeping in mind:

❋ The use of small amounts of gelatin acts as a binder, giving your ice cream better body and smoothness. Eggs, cornstarch, and flour are also good agents of smoothness.

❋ Corn syrup, honey, or other sweeteners may be used to replace sugar.

❋ Evaporated milk can be substituted for whole milk and serves to give the ice cream more heft.

FLAVORING SEMINAR

Imparting flavor to ice cream is a simple but precise art. Vanilla becomes strawberry with the addition of 1 pound per gallon of crushed or sliced strawberries, which are worked into the partially frozen vanilla mix in the freezer can. Chocolate is produced by adding a cup of your favorite chocolate syrup to the mix just as you begin the crank-freezing process or by dissolving 4 squares of cooking chocolate in the vanilla mixture when heating, and adding an extra cup of sugar. The latter produces a much richer chocolate.

Borrowing heavily on the determinations made by Dr. Arbuckle, here is a listing of other kinds of ice cream and the ingredients needed to flavor one gallon of *vanilla* ice cream. Those items marked with one asterisk (*) are to be stirred in only after the mix has been partially frozen and those with a double-asterisk (**) are to be worked in after the ice cream comes out of the crank-freezer and before it is placed in the refrigerator-freezer. All others are to be added to the mix before freezing.

Flavor	*Ingredients*	*Quantities*
BANANA	Bananas (forced through a sieve)	12 *
BUTTER PECAN	Butter	8 tablespoons
	Chopped pecans	1 cup *
	Brown sugar	3 cups (substitute this for sugar in basic mix)
CHOCOLATE CHIP	Grated semi-sweet chocolate	3½ cups *
COFFEE	Instant coffee	6–8 tablespoons (added to *hot* mix)
LEMON	Lemon juice	4 lemons
	Sugar	¾ cup
	Rind gratings	2 lemons *
	Orange juice	2–4 teaspoons

Flavor	Ingredients	Quantities
MARBLE FUDGE	Chocolate syrup	10 ounces ** (more for richer blend)
MOCHA ALMOND FUDGE	Instant coffee	6–8 tablespoons
	Grated almonds	2 cups *
	Chocolate syrup	8–10 ounces **
NUT	Walnuts or pecans	¼ pound *
	Vanilla	1½ tablespoons additional
	Salt	¼ teaspoon
ORANGE	Orange juice	4 oranges
	Lemon juice	1 lemon
	Rind gratings	2 oranges *
	Sugar	½ cup
PEACH	Crushed or sliced peaches	1 pound *
PEPPERMINT	Pulverized peppermint candy	5 ounces *
PINEAPPLE	Crushed pineapple	1 pound *
	Vanilla	¼ tablespoon additional
RASPBERRY	Crushed raspberries	5 ounces *
RUM RAISIN	Ground raisins (seedless)	3 cups *
	Rum	¾ cup (soak raisins in rum before mixing in)

Of course, this is just a fraction of the flavors possible, but with these as examples other flavor possibilities suggest themselves. For example, banana becomes banana nut with the addition of 2 cups chopped nuts, and the substitution of butterscotch

Borden
Malted milk, originated by William Horlick of Racine, Wisconsin, is featured on this Borden's wagon of the 1890s.

for chocolate in the marble fudge listing yields butterscotch ripple. Once you have mastered some of the basic recipes, the urge to experiment often beckons. Some of the items worth having on hand when that urge hits include:

Almond extract
Apricot nectar
Blueberries (strained)
Butter crunch candy
Cake or cookie crumbs (e.g., ladyfingers, sponge cake, etc.—used for making bisque ice cream)
Cinnamon ⎫ (particularly suited to enhance and vary the flavor
Cloves ⎬ of chocolate and coffee ice creams, but only in
Nutmeg ⎭ minute quantities)
Dates
Ginger
Grapenuts (especially good mixed with malted milk powder)
Homemade caramel
Homemade tutti-frutti (equal parts chopped cherries, pineapple, raisins, and nuts; rum can be added)
Licorice
Lime juice
Macaroon crumbs
Mango pulp
Maple syrup, sugar, or extract
Marshmallow (which, additionally, helps to bind the ice cream)
Mint
Mint chocolate chips
Molasses taffy
Nesselrode
Pulverized peanut brittle (as with any hard candy, it must be present in *very small* pieces because frozen hard candy can threaten teeth)
Rum, creme de menthe, or Cherry Heering
Toasted coconut (a double treat when combined with a basic formula in which coconut milk has been used instead of cream)

Persons who have been working in the field for a long time can offer the best rules and hints for the novice. Here are some of those suggestions arranged by flavor category.

NUTS

According to Philip G. Keeney of Penn State's College of Agriculture, "Roasted nuts are less likely to absorb moisture than untreated nuts. Most nut flavors are best when combined with a background flavor such as vanilla, maple or butterscotch." Most authorities agree that a very small quantity of salt should be added to enhance the flavor of nuts.

FRUITS

"Fresh fruit must be considered the best source of flavor," says Arbuckle, who adds that once it is peeled and cut up, one gets best results if it is aged a few hours in sugar—a process that employs osmotic action to create a flavorful syrup around the fruit. This process can be used to advantage with every fruit except the banana and the grape.

COLOR

Save for chocolate, just about every commercial ice cream is artificially colored (including vanilla, which often is spiked with yellow), with almost all of these colors being chemical rather than vegetable. Unless you are hooked on coal-tar derivatives or feel that your strawberry has to be a dark commercial-grade pink instead of light pink, there is no reason to color homemade ice cream—except, perhaps, for the traditional vegetable-green of homemade pistachio. If you must use coloring, it should be added to the liquid mix to ensure uniformity. Colors should also be added sparingly, as the freezing process tends to transform subtle colors into technicolor.

SYRUPS

Arbuckle warns that when sweet syrups are used, the sugar content of the basic mix should be adjusted accordingly. If you use a healthy quantity of, say, maple syrup or honey to flavor your ice cream, the amount of sugar in the basic mix must be cut sharply or even cut out entirely in order to avoid excessive sweetness. This is common sense, but many a batch of homemade ice cream has been ruined because attention was not paid to *balance*. Just as obvious: one would give an extra shot of sugar to an infusion of particularly tart fruit.

ADVANCED FLAVORING TECHNIQUES

Indicative of the innovative side of modern ice cream experts is their ability to create new flavors on demand. Sweet potato ice cream was created by Arbuckle at the request of the Maryland Sweet Potato Growers' Association. It came about after countless experiments, beginning in 1964, and was perfected by Arbuckle and his colleagues in time to debut at the Maryland Pavilion of the New York World's Fair in 1965. Here is the formula for this surprisingly pleasant-tasting curiosity.

Besides puréed sweet potatoes one will need lemon chips, which can be made from pulverizing lemon drops. For a gallon of ice cream add 3 pints of puréed sweet potato to the vanilla mix and 3 ounces of lemon chips to the partially frozen ice cream. If you wish to give this the color of sweet potatoes, add 1½ teaspoons of mixed red and yellow vegetable coloring.

In light of this formula it is interesting to note that ice

cream flavor innovations often occur as a result of finding an ingredient which did not seem appropriate at the beginning of the search. In the case of sweet potato, the search led to lemon as the agent needed to impart the tartness that makes the final product taste good. Similarly, Arbuckle's rhubarb ice cream calls for a pinch of mace and a touch of preserved orange rind to bring out the flavor of the cooked crushed rhubarb.

Still another example of how far one can push flavoring is "Pickles and Ice Cream." This ice cream was created by Miller's Ice Cream Parlor of Eaton Rapids, Michigan, for that town's annual Pickles and Ice Cream Festival—a celebration brought about by the fact that the Miller Dairy and the Heifetz Pickling Company are the pillars of the Eaton Rapids economy. The delicacy has been introduced elsewhere, including southern California where it has become a brisk-selling item as a gift for expectant mothers. For a gallon of this blend you will need 2 tablespoons of dill pickle flavoring and 4 cups of chopped candied pickles. The flavoring is added to the basic vanilla mix and the candied pickle bits are worked into the partially frozen mix.

SHERBETS AND ICES

The freezing procedure for making sherbets and ices is the same as that used in making ice cream except that the ratio of salt to ice in the tub should be 1 part salt to 5 parts ice rather than 1 part salt to 6–8 parts ice. As is true with vanilla mixes, there are a host of sherbet and ice formulas, but these five adapted from University of Illinois and Department of Agriculture recipes should be enough for a basic repertoire.

Allen Rodney Studios
John Bertolini, ice cream sculptor for the Louis Sherry Ice Cream Company in Brooklyn, is one of the last of his breed. He has produced over 100,000 works.

BASIC MIX FOR FRUIT SHERBET
OTHER THAN LEMON
(*about 3 quarts*)

6 *cups milk*

2 *cups sugar*

2½ *cups fruit juice or pulp*

4–8 *tablespoons fresh, frozen, or bottled lemon juice*

¼–½ *teaspoon salt, if desired*

Mix milk and sugar. Add lemon juice to fruit juices or pulp and taste for tartness. Gradually add fruit mixture to milk, stirring constantly. Freeze (remembering to use 1 part salt to 5 parts ice).

NOTE: This sherbet may curdle at first, but when done it is smooth and creamy. For greater smoothness add 2 tablespoons unflavored gelatin that has been softened in cold water and then dissolved over low heat.

Orange sherbet will taste best if you add 2 tablespoons grated orange rind.

LEMON SHERBET (*about 3½ quarts*)

2 *quarts milk*

½ *teaspoon salt*

3 *cups sugar*

1½ *cups lemon juice*

2 *tablespoons grated lemon rind*

Combine milk, salt, and sugar. Stir until sugar is dissolved. Add lemon juice and rind very slowly to milk, stirring constantly. Freeze.

BASIC RECIPE FOR ICES (*makes 1 gallon*)

2 *tablespoons unflavored gelatin*

1 *cup cold water*

4 *cups sugar*

8 *cups fruit juice*

4–8 *tablespoons lemon juice*

Soften gelatin in 1 cup cold water for 5 minutes. Make a hot syrup of the sugar and 2 cups of the fruit juice. Dissolve the softened gelatin in the hot syrup. Add remaining ingredients. Cool before freezing.

NOTE: For sweetened fruit juices, use less sugar; for very tart juices, use more. Be sure to taste juices and add enough lemon juice to make the mixture tart.

BASIC SOUR-MILK SHERBET (about 2 quarts)

4 cups sour milk or buttermilk
2 cups sugar
2 eggs, separated
½ cup water

2 lemons (juice only)
½ cup juice of grape or what-
  ever flavor desired for
  sherbet

Sour milk or buttermilk should be sour enough to curdle. Combine milk and sugar. Cook egg yolks and water to a thin custard. Add beaten egg whites, and combine this mixture with the milk and sugar. Add fruit juices and freeze.

SYRUPS AND TOPPINGS

The final requirement of a fundamental ice cream education is the ability to construct the syrups and toppings essential for ice cream concocting. A simple syrup to be used with fruit extracts can be made by mixing approximately 1 part water to 1 part sugar and heating to dissolve, but not to boil. Combining 11 ounces of sugar and 10 ounces of water yields a pint of this simple syrup, ready for flavoring. When using pure extracts add

¼–½ ounce to each pint or, when using crushed fruit or juice, about 3 ounces. The simplest fruit topping is made by aging crushed fruit in sugar for 12–24 hours in the refrigerator. For strawberry, blueberry, raspberry, and peach the proportion of fruit to sugar is 4 to 1, while the ratio for cherry is 5 to 1 and for apple 7 to 1.

Beyond these simple items, one may wish to make more sophisticated toppings, such as the following that have been worked up in the test kitchens of the National Dairy Council and the American Dairy Association.

CHOCOLATE SAUCE AND VARIATIONS (*2 cups*)

¼ cup butter

2 squares unsweetened chocolate

1½ cups sugar

⅛ teaspoon salt

¾ cup light cream

½ teaspoon vanilla

Melt butter and chocolate over very low heat. Add sugar gradually, blending well. Add salt; stir in cream gradually. Cook 5 to 6 minutes to dissolve sugar. Remove from heat. Add vanilla.

For variations, to 1 cup of basic sauce, add:

1 tablespoon instant coffee, for mocha

⅛ teaspoon almond extract plus ½ cup toasted slivered almonds, for almond chocolate sauce

½ cup crushed peppermint candy, for peppermint chocolate

½ cup cream, whipped (added to cold sauce and served cold), for fluffy chocolate

2 teaspoons grated orange rind, 2 tablespoons orange juice, and ½ teaspoon grated lemon rind, for fruit chocolate.

145

MALLOWBERRY (*1 cup*)

Fold ½ cup whole cranberry sauce into ½ cup marshmallow crème.

SOUR CREAM SAUCE (*1 cup*)

Mix ¾ cup sour cream, ¾ teaspoon cinnamon, ¾ teaspoon nutmeg, and 1 tablespoon sugar.

COFFEE CARAMEL (*1 cup*)

Over boiling water melt ½ pound vanilla caramels with 2 tablespoons milk and 2 teaspoons instant coffee. Serve hot.

CURRANT JELLY (*1 cup*)

In a saucepan blend 2 teaspoons cornstarch and 2 tablespoons lemon juice; add 1 cup currant jelly. Bring to boil over low heat, stirring constantly. Cool.

PRALINE (*2 cups*)

In a saucepan combine 1 cup light brown sugar, ¼ cup light corn syrup, ½ cup half-and-half, and ⅛ teaspoon salt. Add ¼ stick butter. Cook over medium heat, stirring constantly, about 10 minutes or until thick and smooth. Stir in 1 teaspoon vanilla and 1 cup pecan halves.

JAMAICAN MAGIC (*1 cup*)

Toss 1 cup moist, shredded coconut with ¼ cup brown sugar and 1 tablespoon melted butter. Brown in oven. Cool.

The basic ability to make ice creams, sherbets, and a few simple sauces can be complemented with another (many would say higher) skill, namely, that of dispensing ice cream in spectacular combinations and concoctions. About to begin is an advanced course in the ice cream arts in which we will sample some of the great formulas of the past and study some of the skills of the soda jerk.

IX

An Annotated, Chronological Compendium of Concoctions, Constructions, and Conceits —Good Eats!

A REWARD accruing to the ice cream researcher is that, within the moldy texts and dog-eared dairy industry periodicals which are searched, there are formulas and bits of technical derring-do leaping from the musty pages begging to be reintroduced and enjoyed anew in this more complicated era. Rather than hoard this delectable body of knowledge, a selection of fifty or so of these discoveries (plus a few recent innovations) has been assembled in this chapter—many of them have been tested and validated in the author's secret test kitchen.

While this collection represents only a small fraction of the thousands of great concoctions in the literature of ice cream, it is hoped that it is enough to help renew interest in creative concocting and expert soda jerking, whether amateur or professional.

In deference to the historical nature of these formulas, they are presented chronologically, with notes and in the language style in which they were first offered. Before moving on to the tantalizing specifics of the Panama Cooler, Dionne Surprise, Coffee Frappe, and Broadway, it will be necessary to spend a moment discussing the tools of soda jerking.

The formulas that follow refer to scoops by number, ranging from the tiny No. 30 to the imposing No. 12. The number of a scoop indicates the number of portions it will dish from a quart of ice cream: a No. 24 scoop will take twenty-four level scoopfuls. The determined ice cream aficionado will want to be armed with the five basic scoops, listed below. Others will find the sizes helpful in determining the amount of ice cream called for in the formulas.

No. 30, about 1¾ inches in diameter, is normally the scoop for parfaits and ice cream "sampler" bowls.

No. 24, measuring 2 inches in diameter, is the standard scoop for the ice cream cone.

No. 20, 2¼ inches across, is known as the à la mode scoop.

No. 16, 2½ inches across, is the scoop most often used when a bowl of ice cream is ordered.

No. 12, almost 2¾ inches across, is the large scoop used for many sundaes.

While there are literally dozens of examples of ice cream glassware from tiny sherbet cups to large sundae troughs, over the years a basic seven-piece set has emerged to cover most contingencies. They are: the 14-oz. Soda glass (which comes in tapered, straight, and footed versions), the classic Tulip Sundae, the Footed Crimped Sundae, the Banana Split, the Crimped Parfait, Footed Ice Cream Bowl, and the Footed Crimped Twin.*

In concocting the sodas that follow, soda water presents something of a problem for the modern soda jerker, because it is increasingly difficult to gain access to items like the "Super-Soda Draft Arm" of a Bastian-Blessing fountain with its remarkably versatile nozzle action. Given this deplorable situation, your best bet is to obtain soda water in a siphon so that at least some of the heady feeling and mixing action of *spritzkrieg* can be experienced. If one must rely on common bottled soda water, some of the feeling can be attained by shaking the bottle, covering part of its mouth with a thumb, and aiming carefully.

Finally there is the matter of the ice cream itself. Great concoctions require that attention be paid to "holding temperature," namely, that temperature at which ice cream is at its most dippable. This condition is generally defined as that point at which it is firm enough to be cut easily, soft enough so that pressure is not required to fill the dipper, and not so soft as to cause undue shrinkage. The International Association of Ice Cream Manufacturers has determined that this state lies between 8 and 12°F. and goes on to suggest that experimentation is required to determine the exact temperature for different brands, which, of course, have different freezing characteristics.

Now on to the formulary.

---

* The reader is again reminded that sources for obtaining glassware, scoops, toppings, etc., are contained in the appendix.

Library of Congress
Time was when ice cream shops took imaginative shapes like this stand along
a highway near Berlin, Connecticut, which was captured by photographer
Russell Lee in 1939.

THE MAPLE PARFAIT/THE CATAWBA FLIP/WALNUT CREAM SYRUP—1903

Originally published in 1863, *The American Dispenser's Book . . . Containing Choice Formulas for Making Soda Water Syrups and Fancy Drinks, or: How to Make a Soda Fountain Pay* was one of the first of many books to launch the emerging soda fountain industry into sophisticated glory. Many of these original formularies have been lost—eluding even the acquisitive grasp of the Library of Congress—and are known by reputation only. The 1903 edition of *The American Dispenser's Guide . . .* was found, revised, and republished in 1971 as a joint effort of Howard Johnson's and Winter House Ltd. (It sells for $1.95 in bookstores and at Howard Johnson's.) By permission, here are three formulas from the 1903 (1971) edition.

THE MAPLE PARFAIT

If you follow these directions carefully, you will have the most perfect thing ever set out on a soda counter.

4 *eggs, yolks only*	1 *pint heavy cream, well*
¾ *cup maple syrup*	*whipped*

In the top of a double boiler combine beaten egg yolks and maple syrup. Stir over boiling water until mixture thickens and coats a spoon. Remove from fire and cool. Fold whipped cream into the cooled mixture and turn into a mold. Cover tightly and freeze without stirring for 4 or 5 hours. Serve in stem glasses with a spoonful of whipped cream. Serves 6.

THE CATAWBA FLIP

1 *ounce ice cream*   A *sufficient quantity chipped*
1 *ounce grape syrup*   *ice*
1 *egg*

Put all into a shaker, and mix thoroughly. Strain into a glass, fill with soda water, dust some nutmeg over the top, and serve immediately. Sells like hot cakes.

WALNUT CREAM SYRUP

Take 1 pound of walnut kernels and remove the skin by blanching—the skin, if left on, would give an unpleasant, bitter taste; then powder in a Wedgwood or porcelain mortar, adding a few drops of lemon juice to prevent the separation of oil in kernels; water, gradually added, will make a thick emulsion. As fast as the kernels are reduced, put them in a linen cloth, which should be gathered around them so that they may be squeezed through the cloth. Whatever is left in the cloth should be returned to the mortar and pulverized further, the lemon juice and water being added as needed. All should eventually pass through the strainer. The result of this process (about two pints) is to be added to two quarts of cream syrup (which is made by stirring together: 1 quart sweet cream, 1 quart milk, and 4 pounds of sugar).

This formula may be varied, and perhaps improved, by a slight addition of extract of lemon, or vanilla, or any other flavor to suit the taste; likewise a little coloring to suit the fancy. It will repay the labor of preparing it.

NOTE: This syrup recipe is one of the hundreds which appeared in the earlier manuals and one of those which relies on ingredients still generally available. When syrup-making was a great art, its practitioners commonly used such extracts, essences, and elixirs as Phosphate Brain, Pepsin and Iron, Tonic Beer, Blood Orange, Orris Root, Orgeat, Coriander, and Elixir of Calisaya.

THE HOT MAPLE SUNDAE/THE PANAMA COOLER— 1909

The first American soda fountain manual to break into the over-1,000-formula category was the second edition of the *Dispenser's Soda Water Guide* which contained 1,300 concoctions. It provided over one hundred sundae formulas alone, even though that art form was barely a decade old. Revived for today is one of the *Guide's* assortment of hot sundaes and one of its summer coolers.

THE HOT MAPLE SUNDAE

Pour a ladleful of hot maple syrup over a scoop of vanilla ice cream, and over the whole, sprinkle ground hickory nuts. Serve with wafer.

THE PANAMA COOLER

Strawberry syrup	1 *fluid ounce*
Vanilla syrup	1 *fluid ounce*
Vanilla ice cream	1 *tablespoon*
Soda	

Place ice cream in a 12-ounce glass, add the syrups, and fill with carbonated water. Mix.

WHITE'S FLYER/THE ALASKA SNOWBALL—1910

The Liquid Carbonic Company, a leading manufacturer of soda fountains and fountain equipment, periodically published its *Soda Water Guide and Book of Tested Recipes* to go with its hardware. Carbonic's *Guides* sought to show that carbonated waters—or "temperance champagne" as the company called it —could be used to produce all manner of healthful good fun. Here are two typical entries in the 1910 edition of the *Guide*.

WHITE'S FLYER

Put a ladle of vanilla ice cream in a sundae cup; cover over with pecan nuts. Now mix in a separate glass ½ ounce vanilla syrup, 1 ounce sweet cream, and 1 egg. Shake well and pour over ice cream in sundae dish. Garnish with whipped cream and maraschino cherry.

THE ALASKA SNOWBALL

Combine 1 egg, ½ ounce lemon syrup, ½ ounce orange syrup, ½ ounce raspberry syrup, ½ ounce sweet cream, and 1 tumblerful of shaven ice. Shake well in milk shaker and add plain soda to rim.

CHOP SUEY DOUBLE SUNDAE—1913

This is an especially rich selection from *The National Soda Fountain Guide* by William S. Adkins, another of the mammoth formula directories which made the American soda fountain a marvel of gooey diversity.

Take raisins, dates, and figs, in equal quantities; chop them and mix with enough simple syrup* of a heavy grade to permit the mixture to pour easily. This is the chop suey mixture. Now place two large mounds of desired ice cream in a large bowl. Pour a ladle of chop suey mix in a space between the mounds, and top with whole cherry and coconut.

BANANA À LA NEW YORK/NORTH POLE SUNDAE/ COFFEE FRAPPE—1919

The very popular and influential *Spatula Soda Water Guide* was first published in 1901. By the fifth edition, which came out in 1919, it contained over one thousand fountain formulas, including twenty-five banana splits, fifty nut sundaes, a concoction dedicated to every major college and fraternal order (like the Tufts Egg Special and the Yale Shake), and 154 separate syrups. Under the inspired direction of E. F. White, soda editor of the Spatula Publishing Company, this directory carried items with such intriguing titles as the Mahogany Puff, the Glasgow Puff, Pikes Peak, the Chautauqua Flip, the Pacific Snowball, and the Allies Sundae (so named because it included American peanuts, English walnuts, and French macaroons). These three formulas reveal soda-expert White at his most creative.

---

* To make simple syrup: Mix 1 part water with 1 part sugar and boil for 5 minutes.

BANANA À LA NEW YORK

Draw 1 ounce of sweet cream into a 12-ounce glass; add 1 ounce of vanilla syrup; into this, slice ½ banana, add a portion of vanilla ice cream, shake thoroughly, and fill with a fine stream of soda water. Pour without straining into a clean glass and top off with whipped cream and serve with a spoon.

NORTH POLE SUNDAE

On a 6-inch, fine china plate (preferably with a winter design) place a slice of angel cake; around which lay 3 slices of orange. On one place a red cherry, on one a white cherry, and on the other a blue cherry. On the cake put a large cone-shaped scoop of vanilla. In the top of the cone insert a Véronique wafer, allowing one inch of the wafer to appear above the cream, to represent the pole. Place 3 spoonfuls of pineapple around the base between the slices of orange. Put a little whipped cream around the base of the pole. Arrange 4 chocolate "Teddy Bears" around the whipping, so that they appear to be trying to reach the pole (as an alternative to the bears, one may wish to place a small paper American flag atop the pole). Price at $.20.

COFFEE FRAPPE

Serve in a 12-ounce glass: 1½ ounces coffee syrup, the white of 1 egg, 1½ ounces pure sweet cream, and a small portion of fine-shaved ice. Cover with a shaker and shake thoroughly to beat the white of the egg light, and then remove the glass, leaving the contents in the shaker. Now fill the shaker two-thirds full of soda, using the fine stream only. Pour into the glass and back, and then strain into a clean glass. Serve at once and without straws. The drink should be drunk at once, else it will settle and lose its lightness and richness. (This beverage requires much practice.)

THE QUEEN ANNE SUNDAE/THE MARY BROWNE SUNDAE—1923

Two strong sundae trends of the 1920s are illustrated by these two formulas from *Soda Fountain* magazine. The first is a creative concern with new dressings and toppings and the second is a proclivity to name new sundaes after persons of note. Such was the custom of dedicating sundaes that *Soda Fountain* published formulas for concoctions like, ''The Coolidge,'' ''Firpo's Imagination,'' ''Barney Google's Favorite,'' and ''Valentino's Delight.'' The Mary Browne of the second sundae below was an entertainer of the era who had distinguished herself by playing to American troops overseas during World War I.

THE QUEEN ANNE SUNDAE

Take 2 cups sugar, 1 cup water, ½ cup raisins or currants and ½ grated lemon rind. Boil until thick. Cut up 1 banana, 2 peaches, and enough apple to make ½ cup, and add ½ cup chopped nut meats. Mix in with the syrup as prepared above. Use a ladleful of this dressing for one sundae and top with a dash of whipped cream and a cherry.

THE MARY BROWNE SUNDAE

Take 1 pound figs and 2 pounds evaporated [dried] apricots and boil until very soft. Grind fine in a food chopper and add the juice of one lemon and then blend to proper consistency with simple syrup. Use one ladle of this dressing over strawberry and vanilla ice cream. Top with almond-flavored whipped cream and a slice of peach.

MAPLE TEMPTATION SAUCE/THE TUNE-IN SUNDAE/ THE THIRD DEGREE/THE BLACK-EYED SUSAN/ THE PEANUT MALTED—1925

A vital year in literature—*The Waste Land, The Great Gatsby, Manhattan Transfer,* etc.—1925 was also rich in new fountain formulas. Certain 1925 issues of *Soda Fountain* featured over one hundred new formulas, a pace that the magazine never equaled before or after. Here are five classics resurrected from that banner year.

MAPLE TEMPTATION SAUCE

Crushed pineapple, very fine and heavy	1 *quart*
Genuine maple syrup	1 *quart*
Pecan nuts, cut fine	½ *pound*
Undiluted marshmallow	1 *pint*

Whip all together for 10 minutes. Pour ladleful over ice cream.

International Association of Ice Cream Manufacturers
During the earlier part of this century, ice cream trucks were often configured to attract attention to the product. Hendler's Creamery of Baltimore, which is now part of Borden, not only had trucks like this one but others that carried ice cream inside gigantic replicas of ice cream sundaes.

THE TUNE-IN SUNDAE

Soda Fountain billed this one as a sure bet for capturing the student flapper trade.

Serve on a plate 1 slice of brick ice cream, any flavor, covered with a ladleful of marshmallow sauce. On top, place 3 chocolate bonbons at regular intervals to represent the 3 dials of the radio. With brown-colored whipped cream draw small lines from each chocolate center in the manner of an indicator.

THE THIRD DEGREE

Shaved ice	½ *glassful*
Sweet cherry juice	1 *fluid ounce*
Lemon juice	1 *teaspoonful*
Angostura bitters	1 *dash*
Powdered sugar	1 *teaspoonful*

Add 2 ounces of carbonated water, mix, and strain into a cocktail glass; add a cherry and a small slice of lemon peel and serve.

THE BLACK-EYED SUSAN

Fill a tall sundae glass with vanilla ice cream. Pour over this a thin dressing of marshmallow sauce. Garnish with black-eyed Susan—a chocolate in the center, and thin strips of orange or peach arranged in pairs extending downwards from the base of the chocolate.

THE PEANUT MALTED

Beat together: 1 heaping teaspoon peanut butter, 1 ounce simple syrup, 1 No. 12 scoop vanilla ice cream, and 2 teaspoons malted-milk powder.

THE SCIENCE OF PROPER DIPPING—1928

As the ice cream industry bloomed, more and more universities began offering courses in ice cream production. One result of this academic attention was a group of detailed, comprehensive textbooks, among which was *The Ice Cream Industry* by Grover Turbow, Paul Tracy, and Lloyd Rafetto, three professors of dairy sciences. This text and others of its ilk approached virtually every aspect of ice cream production and distribution in the same manner as the definitive set of rules for scientific dipping printed below.

1. Hold the dipper at such an angle that the sharp cutting edge rolls the ice cream into a ball. Avoid compressing the ice cream with the back of the dipper. Never squeeze ice cream into the dipper.

2. The dipper should be held perpendicular to the surface of the ice cream.

3. The force that moves the dipper should be principally in the muscles of your arm and back, not in your wrist.

4. Always move the dipper across and up in the can of ice cream. In other words, "Dip, don't dig."

C. L. TAYLOR'S ALL-PURPOSE CHOCOLATE
BITTERSWEET SYRUP—1928

During the Golden Age of the American fountain, a group of specialists emerged to act as advisers to the nation's corps of soda jerks. Usually they were former jerkers who had risen to fountain management and then to consulting roles with large companies which either produced fountains or sold fountain supplies. One such man was C. L. Taylor, who had risen from jerker to manager of forty Walgreen's fountains to become fountain-services manager for the Ovaltine Corporation. Taylor's forte was chocolate, and he promulgated scores of chocolate-based formulas, including this one for a rich all-purpose (sundaes, sodas, etc.,) syrup. It became very popular and helped lead the nation away from watery chocolate syrups. This formula was intended for a day's supply of syrup at a busy fountain and would require cutting for home use.

18 *ounces good-grade choco-* *late powder—dark in* *roast, high in butterfat*

6½ *pounds pure cane sugar* 3 *pints water* ½ *teaspoon salt*

Mix sugar and chocolate together; whip the mixture slowly into the water to which the salt has been added and which has been brought to the boiling point. Boil from 3 to 5 minutes, mixing all the while.

THE GILCHRIST GINGER ALE HY-BALL—1931

One of the opulent ice cream parlors of the 1930s was the fashionable Gilchrist's Marble Spa in Boston. Its manager, V. D. Hunt, was a fountain innovator of note who kept the Spa packed with Boston notables with simple but out-of-the-ordinary specials like this one, which he divulged to *Soda Fountain* magazine.

Place 5 ounces of ginger ale in a malted-milk shaker; add No. 16 dipper of vanilla ice cream. Stir on mixing machine until ice cream is melted. Serve in 10-ounce glass.

THE ARABIAN COOLER/THE ICE CREAM ENCHILADA —1932

A prime source of new ideas for the ice cream parlor and fountain were the specialized journals which acted as formula exchanges. From the August and September, 1932, issues of *Soda Fountain* come these two formulas, which were rated "prize winners" by the magazine.

THE ARABIAN COOLER
(by M. Brooke, Berkley, Michigan)

Half fill a tall glass with equal parts of thoroughly chilled chocolate drink and extra-strong coffee. Drop in a large scoop of vanilla or maple-nut ice cream. Sprinkle with cinnamon, a dash of cloves, cover with chopped dates and nuts, and top with whipped cream.

THE ICE CREAM ENCHILADA
(*by Helen Lloyd, San Antonio, Texas*)

Cut vanilla ice cream in the shape of a banana and dip in chocolate sauce. Roll in ground nuts and coconut. Then wrap in a large, thin pancake (something that will roll easily and not soak up the liquid). Top with chocolate syrup, whipped cream, ground nuts, and chopped pineapple.

VANILLA POACHED EGGS ON TOAST—1933

Lagging depression-era sales prompted the industry to unveil a variety of bizarre ''sales-stimulating'' ice cream combinations and do-it-yourself suggestions like this one.

Order enough vanilla ice cream to serve the number of guests you have. Cut an ordinary sponge cake to resemble slices of toast and spread a thin layer of vanilla ice cream on top to resemble the white of an egg. Place half a peach or an apricot, round side up, on top and serve.

THE DIONNE SURPRISE—1934

There was a long period when an event or a popular phrase was enough to inspire a fountain concoction, which was then spread across the nation by an alert network of soda jerks. The formulas for many ephemeral creations such as ''The Lindy,'' ''The Airplane Sundaye,'' and ''Flaming Youth'' have been lost, and exist today in name only. However, the sundae created in honor of the Dionne quintuplets comes down to us intact through the work of Harold W. Bentley, who described it in his 1936 article in *American Speech* on the language of the soda jerk.

Place 5 small scoops of vanilla ice cream in a row in a banana-split dish. Top each scoop with a cap of whipped cream and then a cherry. Ladle crushed pineapple on one side of the row and crushed strawberry on the other.

THE "PRECISE" CHOCOLATE MALTED MILK/THE WALDORF PARFAIT—1934

In the days when the corner druggist was called upon to whip up such semimedicinal items as Wahoo Bitters, Tincture of Orris, Compound of Cubear, and Celery Tonic, massive formula books were published to keep him ever ready. Perhaps the most ambitious and far-ranging of these books was the *American Druggist Formula Compendium* of 1934, which contained not only formulas for such compounds and elixirs as those mentioned above, but recipes for such diverse liquids and necessities as Gun Barrel Bluing, Cake Coloring, Marble Tile Patching Compound, Window Defroster, Sunburn Oil, Aluminium Polish, a gas suppressant with the disarming name "Wind Drops," and Cigarette Cure (a mixture of caffeine, sodium bicarbonate, and ginger). This remarkable book also contained several hundred fountain formulas, including the two below—the first billed as the *precise* way to make a chocolate malted and the second allegedly purloined from the Waldorf Astoria for the edification of the druggist in Boise.

THE "PRECISE" CHOCOLATE MALTED MILK

(*a*) Into a malted-milk shaker dispense two ounces of chocolate syrup.

(*b*) Add 2 scraped No. 16 dippers of vanilla ice cream.

(*c*) Add 6 ounces (one Coca-Cola glassful) of milk.

(*d*) Add either 2 level soda spoons or 1 trip of dispenser malted milk.

(*e*) Put in mixer for exactly 1 minute.

(*f*) While drink is mixing, take 10-ounce standard malted-milk glass, put soda spoon of whipped cream inside lip, and place before patron.

(*g*) Take drink off machine, pour 10-ounce glass only ⅔ full, and set shaker by customer to finish at leisure.

THE WALDORF PARFAIT

Into tall parfait glass are placed, in order given, some crushed strawberries, a heaping teaspoon of slightly softened vanilla ice cream, crushed pineapple, a heaping teaspoon of softened strawberry ice cream, crushed raspberries, a spoonful of vanilla ice cream, chopped nuts, whipped cream, and garnish.

THE BANANA SKYSCRAPER—1936 *

The 1930s were big years for the banana split, which was especially popular among the college crowd. The "Skyscraper"

* From *The Ice Cream Review*, July, 1936.

was a famous variation, first served at the Penn Pharmacy near the University of Pennsylvania campus.

½ ounce syrup, any flavor
1 No. 20 or No. 24 scoop vanilla
*   ice cream*
1 banana, quartered

1 No. 20 or No. 24 scoop choco-
*   late ice cream*
1 ounce syrup, any flavor
Whipped cream
½ maraschino cherry

Place one-half ounce syrup in bottom of tall tulip sundae dish. Add scoop of vanilla ice cream. Quarter one ripe banana by cutting once lengthwise and once crosswise. Place quarters upright on ice cream with points of banana upward and cut side next to glass. Place scoop of chocolate ice cream on top of vanilla ice cream between pieces of banana. Cover ice cream with one ounce of syrup, then top with whipped cream and cherry.

THE TECHNOLOGY OF THE CHOCOLATE SODA—1940

So advanced were the fountain arts before World War II that specific drinks and dishes were subject to long technical discussion. One such treatise, entitled "How to Make a Chocolate Ice Cream Soda," appeared in the *Ice Cream Review* for September, 1940. It was written by fountain specialist C. E. Henderson of the Bastian-Blessing Company and contained formulas from all over the nation along with suggestions leading toward perfection in the chocolate ice cream soda. Here is Henderson's basic formula for a 10-cent soda along with a few of those suggestions.

Draw 1½ ounces of chocolate syrup into a sparkling 12-ounce glass.

Fill glass three-quarters full of carbonated water using the fine stream. The glass should be filled to a point where the contents will just come to the brim when the ice cream is added. Some modern glasses have rings around them which make good guides.

By tipping the glass so the carbonated water strikes the side you will avoid splashing and by revolving the glass so that the water flows down on all sides of it, you will mix the water and syrup more thoroughly.

When a glass with a wide top is used, some dispensers use the coarse stream to finish off with, but this is unnecessary if the glass has been filled to the right height with the fine stream. If carbonated water is added after the ice cream, great care must be taken to prevent it from striking the ice cream, as that may break up the ice cream or coat it with ice.

Add one No. 16 dipper of ice cream, slipping it in gently so it will float and be visible when the drink is set before the customer.

HINTS FROM HENDERSON

❀ A sloppy soda that is running over is unpardonable.

❀ For the psychological effect on the customers who may be watching the preparation of the ice cream soda, many operators now use two No. 30 scoops of ice cream instead of one No. 16. Two scoops look larger than one, and it is satisfying to see the dispenser reach into the ice cream can twice.

❀ Some operators now add a soda spoonful of whipped cream, coffee cream or ice cream to the syrup before putting in the charged water. It makes a fluffier soda.

❀ Chocolate Mint Ice Cream Sodas are becoming increasingly popular. These can be made with Crème de Menthe syrup or essence of peppermint. If Crème de Menthe syrup is used . . . one-quarter ounce will be required when a large glass is used. Approximately two drops of peppermint will equal one-quarter ounce of Crème de Menthe syrup in flavoring power. Whichever is used may be put into the glass first, or immediately following the chocolate syrup.

❀ Glamorize the mixing and building of your sodas. Your position behind the counter is comparable to being in a show window. You are an artist demonstrating the right way to mix the perfect Chocolate Ice Cream Soda. Do it deliberately, carefully, artistically. . . .

THE ALL-AMERICAN—1942

This product of the innovative Ice Cream Merchandising Institute was the preferred sundae in the "Victory Sundae" drive of World War II.

Place into a crimp or tulip sundae dish 1 ounce of white marshmallow topping and 2 No. 20 dippers of vanilla ice cream; pour over the ice cream 1 ounce of white marshmallow topping. On the side of the dish, over the marshmallow, place 2 soda spoons of crushed or sliced bright red maraschino cherries and on the other side, over the marshmallow, place 2 soda spoons of fresh or frozen blueberries.

HONEYDEW DIP—1943

Designed by the aforementioned fountain specialist C. E. Henderson, the Honeydew Dip was one of the many wartime

Howard Johnson's
The soda fountain at the original Howard Johnson's. It was in the basement
of this shop that Johnson perfected formulas for twenty-eight flavors of ice
cream. Besides this shop in downtown Wollaston, Massachusetts, Johnson also
ran a stand at Wollaston Beach, where one hot August day he sold 14,000 ice
cream cones.

specials designed around ingredients in short supply or limited through rationing, and it is therefore indicative of the period.

> 1 *dip of lemon ice or sherbet*
> 1 *ring of honeydew melon*

Cut a ripe melon in half midway between the ends and score out the seeds. Slice a ring about ½ inch thick from one of the halves and use as many segments as needed to form a smaller ring around the dip of lemon ice or sherbet. Form a small ring of melon on the ice cream plate, with the ends overlapping, if necessary, so that the hole in the center will be slightly smaller than the dip of ice or sherbet. Then add the dip and serve.

REFRIGERATOR ICE CREAM (PEANUT BUTTER)—1943

To contend with wartime shortages (of heavy cream, sugar, etc.), which made it all but impossible to make homemade ice cream, an array of ersatz refrigerator ice cream formulas were devised and promulgated. Many are best forgotten, but not this sugar-scant offering from the New York *Times* of July 4, 1943.

1½ *tablespoons flour*	½ *cup peanut butter*
¼ *teaspoon salt*	¾ *cup milk*
½ *cup sugar*	2 *egg whites*
¼ *cup cold milk*	2 *tablespoons sugar*
1¾ *cups scalded milk*	1 *teaspoon vanilla*
2 *egg yolks, beaten*	

Set indicator of mechanical refrigerator at coldest point. Blend flour, salt, sugar, and cold milk. Slowly add the scalded milk and boil, stirring constantly, two minutes. Pour slowly over egg yolks and cook, while stirring, in the top of a double boiler about two minutes. Cool thoroughly. Mix peanut butter with milk, and cream until smooth. Blend with cooked custard mixture. Beat egg whites until stiff, add sugar and vanilla, and beat until peaks will form. Fold into cold custard. Pour into tray of mechanical refrigerator and freeze, stirring twice during the freezing period. Serves 8.

THE BLACK COW/THE BROADWAY—1944

Long-established favorites, these two sodas are included under the war years, since this was when they came into their own as GI favorites. The army went to great lengths to get them into the war zone. Here are the preferred formulas.

THE BLACK COW

Root beer syrup	*Vanilla ice cream*
Ice cream, or whipped cream,	*Carbonated water*
or coffee cream	*Whipped cream*

Into a soda glass put 1½ ounces root beer syrup. Add 1 soda spoon whipped cream or ice cream or 1½ ounces coffee cream, and blend. Add fine stream carbonated water until the glass is ¾ full. Float into the carbonated mixture 2 No. 24 dippers vanilla ice cream. If glass is not full, finish filling with coarse stream carbonated water. Top with whipped cream.

173

THE BROADWAY

Chocolate syrup
Ice cream, or whipped cream,
   or coffee cream

Coffee ice cream
Carbonated water
Whipped cream

Procedure same as for the Black Cow, introducing ingredients in the order in which they are listed.

THE MELLOW-CREAM CHOCOLATE SODA—1946

This construction was sufficient to win for Harold Korb of Evansville, Indiana, the title of U.S. Champion Soda Jerker in a contest held in Cincinnati, Ohio. The event was described in Ernie Pyle's *Home Country,* from which the following is quoted.

"His prize number was called the Mellow-Cream Chocolate Soda. Here's how he built it: he put in an ounce and a half of chocolate syrup, then two soda spoons of stiffly whipped cream; he stirred them up very thoroughly and discarded the spoon; he shot a very fine stream of carbonated water into the glass until it was three-quarters of an inch from the top (didn't dare stir it any more); then he plied (yes, plied) two No. 24 dips of ice cream, one gently on top of the other, so it would stick on top of the soda and the customer would see it and say, 'Oh, goody!' "

THE WASHINGTON MONUMENT SUNDAE—1947

Let's Sell Ice Cream was the last of the great ice cream formularies. It was first published in 1947 by the Dairy Training and Merchandising Institute and featured established ice cream classics as well as original creations from specific establishments. One such house specialty was this from Weile's—a long-established parlor of note in the nation's capital.

6 *different flavors of ice cream*	*Whipped cream*
Chocolate syrup	*Candy decorettes (blue and*
Raspberry syrup	*red)*
Nuts in syrup	*Whole cherries*
Bananas	

Into a *very* tall glass put ½ ounce chocolate syrup and 1 No. 30 dipper vanilla ice cream. Add raspberry syrup and 2 or 3 slices of banana. Then continue by alternating with syrups, nuts, and ice creams of different flavors, using a total of 6 dippers of ice cream. Place a half banana upright in center on top, forming the height, and cover with plenty of whipped cream. Sprinkle with red and blue candy decorettes and 5 whole red cherries around the top edge of glass. Insert small American flags.

CRISES JUBILEE—1950

Silas Spitzer, food editor at *Holiday,* explained in his 1950 article on ice cream, "Make Mine Vanilla," that the creation of this classic dish is more ritual than recipe. The ritual according to Spitzer goes like this.

"The performance should take place at table, in full view of the fascinated guests. All you need is a chafing dish, into which you pour the juice from a pint of pitted Bing cherries and bring it to a boil. Thicken the juice with a half teaspoon of cornstarch, dissolved in a little cold water. Add the cherries and heat the mixture for about five minutes, stirring with a large spoon. Pour in two or three ounces of kirsch or good brandy and set ablaze. Serve this sauce with enough vanilla ice cream for six people, ladling it over the individual portions as they are handed around. From such modest histrionics sprouts many a masculine reputation for mastery of the culinary arts.''

THE FLAMING NUT SUNDAE—1950

This particular sundae achieved nationwide prominence when the Associated Press reported it was banned as a fire hazard by officials in Pittsfield, Massachusetts.

The Pittsfield sundae consisted of ½ pint ice cream, 1½ ounces hot fudge, 1 ounce marshmallow, and a liberal sprinkling of nuts. The flame was made possible by dipping a small cube of sugar in lemon extract (alcohol content 70 percent or over). After placing the cube on a banana slice atop the sundae it was lit with a match.

APRICOT ALASKA PIE/TRIPLE ICE CREAM BOMBE WITH FLUFFY CHOCOLATE-NUT SAUCE/STRAWBERRY MOUSSE/CHOCOLATE ICE CREAM ROLL WITH SPECIAL CHOCOLATE SAUCE
—CIRCA 1960

As the fountain went into decline and concocting became less of a fountain art, the creative pendulum swung to the American kitchen where elaborate frozen desserts became more popular. Aiding the trend has been the Thursday-newspaper food section where ''canned'' articles on ice cream desserts appear with regularity, supplying some of the textual material that keeps supermarket ads from running over each other. A prime canner of such "articles" is the American Dairy Association, which researches them in its Chicago test kitchen and then presents them to papers replete with pictures, captions, headline, and exclusive area rights to the piece for a year. This practice, employed by other large food promotion groups, has all of the journalistic authenticity of the televised Bayer Aspirin press conference, but it has produced some good formulas, such as these four from the ADA's arsenal of "articles."

APRICOT ALASKA PIE

Nut-Crumb Crust:
1¼ cups graham cracker
    crumbs (*14 squares*)
¼ cup finely chopped nuts
2 tablespoons sugar
¼ cup (½ stick) butter,
    melted

Filling:
2 pints vanilla ice cream

½ cup apricot preserves
1 teaspoon lemon juice

Meringue Topping:
2 cups (¼ pound) marsh-
    mallows
2 tablespoons apricot pre-
    serves
2 egg whites
¼ cup sugar

To prepare crust: In a small bowl combine crumbs, nuts, sugar and butter; press mixture evenly and firmly against bottom and sides of a 9-inch pie plate, building up around rim. Freeze.

    To fill: Spoon ice cream into shell; spread to edge and level top. Freeze. Mix lemon juice with preserves; spread over ice cream. Freeze.

    To prepare topping: In a 1-quart saucepan heat marshmallows and preserves over very low heat, stirring constantly, until smooth. In a small mixing bowl beat eggs until frothy; gradually add sugar and beat until stiff peaks form. Fold in marshmallow mixture. Mound on pie crust, sealing to crust. Place pie on board. Bake in a preheated 450° oven 2 to 3 minutes or until lightly browned. Serve immediately.

TRIPLE ICE CREAM BOMBE WITH FLUFFY CHOCOLATE-NUT SAUCE

1½ *cups vanilla wafer crumbs* (*40 wafers*)

¼ *cup* (½ *stick*) *butter, melted*

1 *pint vanilla ice cream, softened*

1 *pint chocolate ice cream, softened*

1 *pint New York cherry ice cream, softened*

In a small bowl combine crumbs and butter; press evenly against bottom and sides of 6-cup mold to about ½ inch from top. Freeze. Spread vanilla ice cream evenly with back of spoon over crumb shell. Freeze. Repeat with chocolate ice cream. Freeze. Spoon in New York cherry to fill mold. Freeze. Unmold by dipping into warm water and turn out onto chilled plate. Makes 10 to 12 servings.

Serve with Fluffy Chocolate-Nut Sauce, which is prepared as follows:

1 *package* (*6 ounces*) *semi-sweet chocolate pieces*

1 *cup whipping cream*
½ *cup chopped nuts*

In a small saucepan combine semi-sweet chocolate pieces and ½ cup whipping cream. Heat over low heat, stirring constantly, until chocolate melts and mixture is smooth. Cool. Whip remaining cream; fold into chocolate mixture along with nuts. Yield: approximately 2 cups.

STRAWBERRY MOUSSE

1 *pint strawberries, sliced*
½ *cup sugar*
Water
1 *package (3 ounces) straw-
  berry-flavored gelatin*

1 *pint vanilla ice cream*
½ *cup flaked coconut*
½ *cup finely chopped pecans*
*Sweetened sliced straw-
  berries*

Into a bowl, toss sugar and strawberries; let stand at room temperature at least 1 hour, tossing occasionally; drain and reserve juice. Add sufficient water to strawberry juice to make 1 cup. Bring liquid to boiling. In a bowl pour boiling liquid over gelatin; stir until dissolved. Spoon ice cream into hot gelatin mixture; stir until melted. Cool; when partially thickened, whip in a mixing bowl at highest speed for about 2 minutes. Fold in strawberries, coconut, and pecans. Arrange strawberries in bottom of 4-cup mold to conform to design. Turn mixture into mold; chill until firm. Garnish with additional strawberries. Makes 6 to 8 servings.

CHOCOLATE ICE CREAM ROLL WITH
SPECIAL CHOCOLATE SAUCE

¾ *cup sifted flour*
⅓ *cup cocoa*
¼ *teaspoon salt*
5 *egg whites*
1 *cup sugar*

5 *egg yolks*
1 *tablespoon lemon juice*
2 *tablespoons cocoa*
1 *quart vanilla ice cream,
  softened*

Butter a 15- by 10½- by 1-inch jelly-roll pan; line with waxed paper. Butter paper lightly; set aside. Sift flour, ⅓ cup cocoa, and salt together 2 times; set aside. Beat egg whites just until frothy; gradually add sugar, continuing to beat until stiff. Beat egg yolks with lemon juice until thick and lemon-colored; fold into egg whites. Fold in dry ingredients; pour into pan. Bake in preheated 350° oven 15 to 18 minutes. Sift 2 tablespoons cocoa over a towel. Loosen cake from sides of pan; invert on towel. Remove waxed paper; trim away crusts. Roll up in towel, starting at narrow end; cool on rack. Unroll and remove towel. Spread with ice cream; re-roll. Wrap in freezer-wrap; freeze. Makes 10 servings.

Slice and serve with Special Chocolate Sauce, prepared as follows:

1 *cup (6 ounces) semi-sweet chocolate pieces*

½ *cup whipping cream*
½ *teaspoon vanilla*

In a saucepan over low heat melt chocolate pieces in whipping cream; stir until blended smooth. Remove from heat; stir in vanilla. Serve warm or cold. Yield · 1 cup.

Sauce may be stored in covered container in refrigerator for several days. Sauce may thicken during storage. Before serving, thin with a small amount of cream or milk.

HICKS'S HOT ICE CREAM SODA—1964

A product of the world-famous H. Hicks of Manhattan, a pace-setting establishment which boasts that it has served over two thousand distinct ice cream concoctions—not including those "specials" to which W. C. Fields added nips of his own ingredients and which ultimately got him banned from the place. The parlor's long-standing offer to create new items on demand produced this drink when Burgess Meredith requested a hot ice cream soda. The formula was given to Clementine Paddleford and first appeared in the New York *Herald-Tribune*.

1 *cup fresh hot coffee*	1 *tablespoon whipped heavy*
¼ *cup cocoa*	*cream*
1 *scoop ice cream*	

Into blender pour hot coffee over cocoa and blend. Pour over ice cream in soda glass (keep spoon in glass). When ice cream floats to top, add whipped cream.

THE BUTTERSCOTCH MALTED/THE RAINBOW PARFAIT/COFFEE ROON—1968

In 1968 the Dairy Training and Merchandising Institute brought out a new edition of *Let's Sell Ice Cream,* the modern bible of ice cream merchandising. It was a shorter paperbound edition of the 1947 blockbuster version, and was made available as a result of increasing demand by ice cream sellers for a major retrospective of largely forgotten concoctions. From that 1968 edition come these three ice cream classics.

THE BUTTERSCOTCH MALTED

Cold pasteurized milk	*Butterscotch syrup*
Butterscotch ice cream	*Malted-milk powder*

Into a cold mixing cup put 6 ounces of cold milk. Add 1½ ounces of butterscotch syrup, 2 No. 24 dippers of butterscotch ice cream, and 1 soda spoon of malted-milk powder. Place on the mixer long enough to blend thoroughly. Fill a whipped-cream-dotted, thin shell glass ¾ full and serve the mixing can at the side for over-pour.

THE RAINBOW PARFAIT

Into a Pilsner glass put a soda spoon of chopped or crushed red cherries, add 1 No. 30 dipper of vanilla ice cream—top with a soda spoon of either crushed pineapple, green pineapple, or green shredded coconut. Add 1 No. 30 dipper of chocolate ice cream or the monthly featured flavor of ice cream or sherbet. Cover with crushed strawberries, or with blueberries, raspberries, or some fruit that will blend with the ice cream used. Now add a No. 30 dipper of strawberry ice cream and cover with diced roasted almonds or chopped nuts. Cover in ribbon fashion with whipped cream and garnish with a cherry or a cube of pineapple, or sprinkle with coconut or chocolate bits.

COFFEE ROON

Coffee ice cream	*Whipped cream*
Macaroon crumbs	*Pineapple cube*

Into a crimped sundae dish put 1 spoon macaroon crumbs (macaroons are easily crumbled if allowed to dry for about 1 day). Add 2 No. 20 dippers coffee ice cream. Cover with a generous portion of macaroon crumbs. Top with whipped cream and garnish with a pineapple cube.

This sundae can be made using maple or chocolate ice cream. Change name according to the flavor of ice cream used.

HOW TO EAT AN ICE CREAM CONE—1968

While there is a wealth of technical guidance associated with the creation and presentation of ice cream, little has been written about its consumption. This oversight was partially remedied by writer L. Rust Hills in the August 24, 1968, issue of *The New Yorker* in the article "How to Eat an Ice Cream Cone." It must be read in its entirety to be truly appreciated, but here is a small sampler from Hills's breakthrough work. It is hoped that the appearance of the quotation in the technical section of this book will serve to offset the influence of *The Reader's Guide to Periodical Literature,* whose haughty editor/indexers list the work under the heading "Facetiae."

"In trying to make wise and correct decisions about the ice-cream cone in your hand, you should always keep the objectives in mind. The main objective, of course, is to get the cone under control. Secondarily, one will want to eat the cone calmly and with pleasure. Real pleasure lies not simply in eating the cone but in eating it *right*. Let us assume that you have darted to your open space [reference to dripping-problem areas] and made your necessary emergency repairs. The cone is still dangerous—still, so to speak, 'live.' But you can now proceed with it in an orderly fashion. First, revolve the cone through the full three hundred and sixty degrees, snapping at the loose gobs of ice cream; turn the cone by moving the thumb away from you and the forefinger toward you, so the cone moves counterclockwise. Then, with the cone still 'wound,' which will require the wrist to be bent at the full right angle toward you, apply pressure with the mouth and tongue to accomplish overall realignment, straightening and settling the whole mess. Then, unwinding the cone back through three hundred and sixty degrees, remove any trickles of ice cream. From here on, some supplementary repairs may be necessary, but the cone is now defused.''

BANANA SPLIT PIE—1970

This is the formula for one of those luscious items that show up in the display cases of Baskin-Robbins shops. It appeared in *Scoops,* the B-R dealer magazine, and won the coveted Baskin-Robbins engraved Golden Scoop for its designer, who is Martha Hunter of Columbus, Ohio.

9-inch graham cracker pie shell

8 ounces fresh strawberry ice cream

8 ounces chocolate ice cream

8 ounces vanilla ice cream

1 banana

Crushed pineapple

Chocolate syrup

Crushed almond bits

Maraschino cherries

1. Slice slightly more than half of the banana and lay slices in bottom of pie shell.
2. Place layer of strawberry ice cream on banana slices and smooth.
3. Let freeze for 30 minutes.
4. Remove from freezer and smooth layer of chocolate ice cream on top of the strawberry ice cream.
5. Place layer of crushed pineapple on top of chocolate and let freeze for another 30 minutes.
6. Remove from freezer and smooth on layer of vanilla ice cream. Freeze for 30 minutes.

7. Slice rest of banana and place on top of vanilla ice cream. Dribble chocolate syrup throughout the banana slices. Spear a maraschino cherry through each banana slice. Sprinkle with 1 ounce crushed almond bits.

8. Freeze for 30 minutes.

THE STRAWBERRY THICKSHAKE—1971

Produce associations—ranging from the walnut growers to the cocoa lobby—have increasingly seen the value of plumping for the use of their products in ice cream concoctions and have helped push for this by promoting their own formulas. One of the most active of these has been the California Strawberry Advisory Board, which has come up with a variety of suggestions including this one.

> *Fresh strawberries 1 cup*
> *Vanilla ice cream (softened) 1 cup*

Purée strawberries in blender, add ice cream and blend until smooth. Spoon into tall glass, top with whole strawberry for garnish. Serve immediately with long spoon.

Variations: for Strawberry Thickmalt add 1 tablespoon malted-milk powder, and for Double Strawberry Thickshake use strawberry ice cream.

TOWARD THE REEMERGENCE OF AN ART—(1972)

As the final entry in this compendium of ice cream arts and sciences, here is a group of customs, caveats, amenities, and suggestions which have been culled from a variety of sources. They

Baskin-Robbins
One of the earliest Baskin-Robbins stores. This one opened in 1946 in Burbank, California. Baskin-Robbins' annual sales are now $59 million.

are presented here for the ice cream buff ever alert to improve-
ments in the state of his art. Many go far back before the time
of convenience foods and computer-determined portion control,
when soda jerking was a craft of the first order. The first item,
for example, was a pleasant national amenity of the 1930s that
has been too long neglected.

❀ Nutmeg is to a good malted milk what salt is to soup.
Serve a nutmeg shaker with every shake or malted.

❀ Flat ice cream sodas are disappointing and never satisfying. A good test of carbonated water is to drop a mothball into
a glass of it. If the mothball rises to the surface, the water is of
soda quality.

❀ The true science of dispensing lies in always having your
dishes come out the same.

❀ Don't mix carbonated drinks with a spoon unless it is
unavoidable, as it only tends to liberate the gas. Try to do all mixing with the jerk of soda handle.

❀ The thoughtful dispenser will always stand tumblers up-
side-down in ice so that they will stay cold, ready for refreshment.

❀ Never put shaved ice in ice cream drinks.

❀ A good original name combined with a good original concoction is a strong combination.

❀ Fruit syrups and fruit toppings should be made fresh
each day with fresh ingredients.

❀ Don't use too much syrup. It can make for a sickening
drink.

❀ The finest concoction loses its charm if indifferently
served.

❀ Never refuse anyone a glass of water. Today's water customer is tomorrow's soda customer.

❈ As a soda jerk, don't think of yourself as an automaton. Develop a style and grace of your own. For starters, you may wish to create your own way to break an egg (a one-handed ritual, perhaps) or get a scoop of ice cream into a dish (dive-bomb, toss, or whatever).

❈ If you prefer velvety, thick milk shakes and malts, never pummel your mixture with an egg beater or electric mixer with large blades. These drinks are aerated blends and for that reason come out thick and subtle when made with a blender set to a low speed or with an electric mixer laboring on with a very small blade.

❈ As simple as it sounds, one of the prime secrets of the great soda jerks of yore was the parlay of *very cold* milk (as close to 32° as possible without freezing), *chilled* syrups and toppings (below 50° at least), cold soda (34° to 38°) and ever-so-slightly soft ice cream. If, for example, the milk is not very cold, you will not get the "fluff" that makes shakes and malts so pleasing. Needless to say, hot syrups must be kept warm but not too hot. *Really hot* fudge soon separates and crystallizes.

❈ Soft ice cream that has been rehardened loses some of its texture and develops ice particles. If it is to be used, save it for a shake or a malted.

❈ When experimenting with new dishes, always take notes and make diagrams. Many a great combination has been lost because this simple rule was not obeyed.

❈ A dirty scoop is a sin.

❈ Ice cream should be stored at 0°F. or colder. Keep carton tightly closed. To avoid crystallization after carton has been partially used, cover surface of ice cream with protective wrap. For periods of long storage, enclose carton in freezer wrap.

❀ There is a correct position for a banana in a banana split : the cut side of the banana (with seeds exposed) should be placed in the glass dish in such a way as to be visible to the recipient, thus arousing his or her appetite.

APPENDIX:

What Obtains—A Buyer's Guide to Ice Cream Needs and Equipment

SOME ICE CREAM basics such as ice cream itself, cones, sprinkles, and chocolate syrup are easy to find, while others are not. Here are some suggestions on how to get hold of these harder-to-find items:

GLASSWARE

Authentic soda fountain glassware is hard to find outside of restaurant-supply houses; however, Sears Roebuck offers a basic 12-piece beginner's set for $6.49, which contains 4 banana split dishes, 4 soda glasses, and 4 tulip sundae dishes. For the

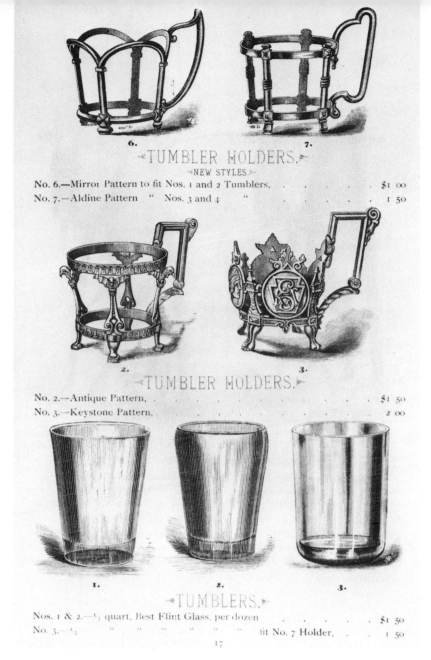

TUMBLER HOLDERS.
NEW STYLES.

No. 6.—Mirror Pattern to fit Nos. 1 and 2 Tumblers, ... $1 00
No. 7.—Aldine Pattern " Nos. 3 and 4 " 1 50

TUMBLER HOLDERS.

No. 2.—Antique Pattern, ... $1 50
No. 3.—Keystone Pattern, ... 2 00

TUMBLERS.

Nos. 1 & 2.—¹⁄₃ quart, Best Flint Glass, per dozen $1 50
No. 3.—¹⁄₃ " " " " " fit No. 7 Holder, . 1 50

17

The New-York Historical Society
As evidenced by this page from the Chas. Lippincott and Co.
catalog of 1880, the tumbler and its holder came in great variety.
Expensive and elaborate holders were just part of the manufacturer's steady drive to induce merchants to "buy up" and em-
bellish their soda operations.

more ambitious, the following firms still make soda fountain glassware and should be able to help you:

Anchor Hocking Glass Corp.
109 North Broad St.
Lancaster, Ohio 43130

Federal Glass Co.
555 Woodrow Ave.
Columbus, Ohio 43207

Indiana Glass Co.
717 E. St.
Dunkirk, Indiana 47336

HOME FREEZERS

There is considerable variety in home freezers on the market today, ranging in price from around $10 for simple hand-crank models to $130 for an elaborate electric number from Abercrombie and Fitch. Aside from new models available at such predictable places as hardware stores, Sears Roebuck and Hammacher Schlemmer, older models crop up in antique stores where the going price for such vintage hand-crankers as Arctic, Fre-Zee-Zee, and White Mountain is between $5 and $15. Though handsome, these freezers are risky investments, since even a touch of internal rust can ruin the ice cream, replacement parts are all but impossible to come by, and the old wooden buckets tend to leak profusely (although soaking the bucket in water for several hours before using can swell the staves and overcome this problem).

The major considerations when selecting a tub are, first,

between electric and hand-crank models and, then, between plastic (or fiberglass) and wood. The advantage of the more costly electric ones is obvious, but the plastic *vs.* wood question is harder to resolve. Plastics are not as well insulated as wood, but the wooden freezers are prone to leak and require more care. Two firms offering broad lines of freezers are:

The Richmond Cedar Works Manufacturing Corp.
400 Bridge St.
Danville, Virginia 24541

The J. E. Porter Co.
Ottawa, Illinois 61350

ICE CREAM CARTS

Ding Dong Cart Co.
95 Chicopee St.
Chicopee, Massachusetts

ICE CREAM MOLDS, OLD-FASHIONED

Fancy molds in all sizes and shapes—ranging from heads of presidents to steam locomotives—used to be extremely popular. A few firms still sell molded ice cream, and one of the early manufacturers of molds is still doing business and will send you a catalog for $2. Write to:

Fr. Krauss' Son
Eighth St.
Milford, Pennsylvania 18337

ICE CREAM PARLOR FURNITURE, OLD-FASHIONED

Simpson-Bosworth Co.
2531–39 North Ashland
Chicago, Illinois 60614

SCOOPS

Many of the older scoops with their rare-wood handles and finely wrought heads are minor works of art worth tracking down. Such classics as the Benedict Indestructo, the Myers De-Luxe Chromium Disher, the Gilchrist Pyramid, and the Arnold 51 often show up in antique shops and white-elephant sales. The author—who possesses a Gilchrist 31, a long, stately throw-out scoop of the 1920s with a German silver head and ejecting spring of phosphor bronze—is partial to the feel and balance of such older models, but this is a personal prejudice. There are many inexpensive scoops on the market today which are easily found in 5 & 10s and supermarkets, as well as professional scoops. Contemporary makers of the latter include:

Roll Dipper Co.
207 Conant St.
Maumee, Ohio 43537

Wilpet Tool and Mfg. Co.
244 Dukes St.
Kearney, New Jersey 07032

Bloomfield Industries Inc.
4546 West 47th St.
Chicago, Illinois 60632

Van Schaack Premium Corp.
566 West Lake St.
Chicago, Illinois 60605

SODA FOUNTAINS AND DIPPING CABINETS

For those wanting to go all the way, these addresses may come in handy:
Grand Rapids Cabinet Co.
56 Baldwin Ave.
Jersey City, New Jersey 07306

Bastian-Blessing Co.
Food and Beverage Equipment Division
4201 Peterson Ave.
Chicago, Illinois 60646

Liquid Carbonic Corp.
4400 West 45th St.
Chicago, Illinois 60632

Mile High Equipment Corp.
545 Santa Fe Drive
Denver, Colorado 80204

Index

"Abuse of the American Hamburger, The," 54

Adkins, William S., 155

Alaska Snowball, 155

Alexander the Great, 15

All-American, 170

Allen, Fred, 81

All-Purpose Chocolate Bittersweet Syrup—1928, C. L. Taylor's, 163

American Dairy Association, 145

American Dispenser's Book, The . . . Containing Choice Formulas for Making Soda Water Syrups and Fancy Drinks, or, How to Make a Soda Fountain Pay, 152

American Druggist Formula Compendium (1934), 166

American Food Laboratories, 115

American Journal of Public Health, 120

American Language, Supplement II, The, 102

"America's typical food," 33

Apricot Alaska Pie, 177–178

Arabian Cooler, 164

Arbuckle, Dr. Wendell, 111, 112, 123, 124, 128, 135, 139, 141

L'Art de Faire des Glaces, 18

Art of Cookery Made Easy, The (1747), 18

Astaire, Fred, 40

Avayou, David, 68, 70

Avignone Frères (Washington, D.C.), 10

Bailey's and Cabot's (Boston), 6, 10

Banana à la New York, 157

Banana Skyscraper—1936, 167–168

Banana split, 33, 36, 60
    tip for preparation of, 189

Banana Split Pie—1970, 184

Barricini candy, 4, 6, 13

Basic Mix for Fruit Sherbet Other Than Lemon, 143

Basic Mix for Ices, 143

Basic Sour Milk Sherbet, 144

Baskin, Burt, 48

Baskin-Robbins Ice Cream, 4, 6, 12, 48, 58, 184

  "largest ice cream sundae," 125

  original flavors, 124–125

Bassett's (Philadelphia), 10

Baur's (Denver), 61

Beatrice Foods, 57

Beecher, Henry Ward, 100

Beethoven, Ludwig von, 20

Bentley, Harold W., 100, 102, 166

Bergman, Torbern, 86

Black Cow, 173

Black-eyed Susan, 161

Bladen, William, 20

Bootleggers, ice cream, 39–40

Bonaparte, Napoleon, 89

Brazelton, Perry, 29, 31

Bresler's (Chicago), 6, 12, 58

  flavor innovations at, 125

Brillat-Savarin, Anthelme, 22

Brimer, Tom, 79

Broadway, 174

Burt, Harry, Jr., 77

Burt, Harry, Sr., 77, 79, 85

Business Week, 9, 39, 43, 81

Butler, Lawson D. ("Two Quart"), 56, 57

Butterscotch Malted, 181–182

Caesar, Nero Claudius, 17

Caffé Florian (Venice), 19

Café Napolitain (Paris), 19

Café Procope (Paris), 19

California Strawberry Advisory Board, 185

Calls, soda jerking, *See* Jargon

Cantor, Eddie, 40

Carbonic-acid gas, 86, 87, 89

Carnation Milk Company, 56

Carts, ice cream, where to buy, 193

Castro, Fidel, 125

Catawba Flip, 153

Centennial, ice cream industry, 51–52

Cerises Jubilée—1950, 175–176

Charles I, King of England, 18

Chile, ice cream in, 36

Chilling, Hippocrates on, 15

China, ice cream in, 36

"Chocolate Enchilada," 94

Chocolate Ice Cream Roll with Special Chocolate Sauce, 179–180

Chocolate Sauce and Variations, 145

Chocolate Shop (Kalamazoo), 10

Chocolate Soda, 168–169

Chop Suey Double Sundae—1913, 155–156

Civil War, ice cream in, 44

Columbia Pictures, 42, 81

Coffee Caramel, 146

Coffee Frappé, 157–158

Coffee Roon, 182

Coney Island, 70

"Confessions of an Ice Cream Eater," 12

Consumer Bulletin, 111, 115

Coltelli, Francesco Procopiodei (Procope), 19

Index

"Comin' Through the Rye," 39

Cornucopia Waffle Company, 70

Craft, Mrs. Carrie Fussell, 52

Crawley, Paul S., 36

"Cream Machine for Making Ice," 22, 24

Creamsicle, 85

Crème frez, 18

"Creme ice," 18

Cuba, ice cream in, 125

Currant Jelly, 146

Curtis, Tony, 52

Custard, frozen, 38

Customs, making and serving ice cream, *See* Tips

Dairy and Ice Cream Field, 115, 117, 120

Dairy Training and Merchandising Institute, 174, 181

Darrow, Clarence, 94

Deering Ice Cream Shops (New England), 6, 119

Depression, Great, 38–40, 73

Dionne quintuplets, 165–166

Dionne Surprise, 165–166

Dipper Dan (Atlanta), 12

Dipping, 162

Dipping cabinets, where to buy, 195

Disney, Walt, 56

Disneyland, ice cream parlor at, 56

Dispenser's Soda Water Guide. 154

Dixie Cup, 59

Dixie Picture Lids, 56

Doumar, Abe, 68–70

Doumars (Norfolk, Virginia), 70

Dows, Gustavus D., 91

Drugstores, *See* Soda fountains

Dubelle, G. H., 63

Durand, Elié Magliore, 89

Eat, Drink and Be Wary, 120

Ecuador, ice cream in, 38

Emerson, Ralph Waldo, 27

Emy, M., 19

Epperson, Frank, 83, 85

Epsicle, 83

"Eskimo Jug," 76

"Eskimo Machine," 76

Eskimo Pie, 36, 59, 60, 73–76

"Essential foodstuff," ice cream as, 45

Everything You Always Wanted to Know About Sex But Were Afraid to Ask, 9–10

Exchange Coffee House (New Orleans), 25

Fair Packaging and Labeling Act, 112

Farrell's (Toledo-based chain), 12

"Father of the American ice cream industry," 31

Federal Bureau of Investigation, 56–57

Federal standards for ice cream, 115, 116, 119

Federal Trade Commission, 83

Fields, W. C., 180–181

Fighting Blood (film serial), 97

Film, ice cream and, 40, 42, 47, 97

Flaming Nut Sundae—1950, 176

"Flapper's Experience," 94

Flavoring, ice cream, 120

   failures, 123

   innovations, 122–126

   in Nero's time, 17

   sales by, 121–122

   unusual, 50, 58–59

"Floating ice cream parlor," 48

Food and Drug Administration, 111, 115

Foremost Dairy, 46, 57

France, ice cream in, 17, 19, 69

Fraser, Sir John, 95

Freezers, 27, 128, 130

   floor, 58

   hand-cranked, 25

   "home," where to buy, 192–193

   self-service, 54, 56

Freezing process (homemade ice cream), 130–131

French Vanilla (Rich) Ice Cream Mix, 132

Furniture, ice cream parlor, where to buy, 194

Fussell, Jacob, 29, 31, 44, 51, 52

Gay Divorcée, The, 40

Germany, ice cream in, 69

Ghiradelli Soda Fountain (San Francisco), 6

Gifford's (Washington, D.C.), 10

Gilchrist Ginger Ale Hy-Ball—1931, 164

Gilchrist's Marble Spa (Boston), 164

Glasse, Hanna, 18

Glassware, where to buy, 190, 192

Godey's Lady's Book, 26

Goldberg, Max, 69

Good Humor bar, 73

Good Humor Corporation of America, 59, 77, 79, 81, 83

   film made about, 81

   flavor innovations at, 125

Good Humor Ice Cream Sucker, 77

Good Humor Man, The (film), 81

Great Britain, ice cream in, 17–18, 49

"Great Malted Milk Defection, The," 54

Green, Robert M., 61, 63, 91

Green, Robert M. and Sons, 63

Greene, Gael, 4, 9, 111, 116

Häagen-Dazs ice cream, 57

Haller, Donald, 97, 99

Hamilton, Mrs. Alexander, 22

Hamwi, Ernest A., 66–68, 70

Health, Education and Welfare, Dept. of, 73

Heifetz, Jascha, 81, 83

Henderson, C. E., 168–169

Hennerich, George W., the "Human Dynamo of the Ice Cream Industry," 43

Henri II, King of France, 17

Henry V, King of England, 18

Hersch, Ralph, 97

Hicks, H. (Manhattan), 4, 180

Hicks's Hot Ice Cream Soda—1964, 180–181

Hills, L. Rust, 183

"Hints from Henderson," 169–170

Hippocrates, 15

History of the Soda Fountain Indus-try, 61
"Hokey-Pokey" (1872), 83
Holbrook, Stewart H., 64
Hollywood, 40, 81
"Hollywood Lunch," 40
Honeydew Dip—1943, 170, 172
Hood, H. P. and Sons, 4
Hot Maple Sundae, 154
Howard, Jane, 12
Howard Johnson's, 4, 6, 152
"Howdy Doody Cake Roll," 56
"How to Eat an Ice Cream Cone,"
    183–184
"How to Make an Ice Cream Soda,"
    168
Humpty-Dumpty episodes, 56
Hutchinson, F. D., 31

Ice, Dry, 76
Ice cream
    additives in, 109–111, 115, 116
    advertisements of, 20–22, 25, 72,
        115, 116
        first public advertisement, 20
    air in, 54, 110, 113
    butterfat in, 54
    caloric value of, 109
    consumption of (U.S.), 8, 28, 36,
        50–51, 54, 74, 76–77
    "economy," 111
    emulsifiers in, 110–111, 115
    flavoring of, *See* Flavoring
    food value of, 109
    "hand packed," 112
    "high quality," 111

Ice Cream (*continued*)
    history of, 14–59
        early history, 14–27
        later history (mid-nineteenth cen-
            tury to present), 28–59
    formulas for, 18–19, 49–50
        commercial formulas, 110
    "French" ice cream, 112
    homemade, 127–147
        color in, 139
        flavoring in, 139–141
        fruit in, 139
        ingredients to have on hand, 138
        nuts in, 139
    industry, American, 28–59
        Washington lobby, 115
    ingredients of, 109–126
        "natural" ingredients, 116
    labeling, lack of requirements for,
        112–115
    overrun in, 54
    "private labels," 54
    sanitation in manufacture of, 119–
        120
    shipping of, 76
    "skirt" in, 58
    stabilizers in, 54, 110–111, 115, 119
    "superior" brands, definition of,
        117–119
    symbolic value of, 49, 59
    technology, 120
Ice Cream, 111, 112, 124
Ice cream cone, 66–73, 85
"Ice Cream Cone Revisited, The," 68
"Ice Cream Congress," 59
Ice Cream Enchilada, 165
Ice cream float, 60

Ice Cream Industry, The, 162

"Ice cream Marines," 45

Ice Cream Merchandising Institute, 43, 50, 170

Ice-cream-on-a-stick, 61, 85

Ice cream parlors, 25, 36, 48, 56, 58

Ice cream poisoning, 120

Ice Cream Review, The, 33, 35, 38–39, 42, 49, 51, 65, 72, 83, 167, 168

Ice cream sandwich, 60, 73

Ice cream soda, 33, 60, 61, 63, 64, 85, 91–92

Ice cream sundae, 33, 50, 60, 64–66, 85

"Ice Cream Telegram," 42

Ice Cream Trade Journal, 33

Ice Cream World, 116

"Ice harvesting," 25

Icehouses, 25

Illinois, University of, ice cream recipes, 141–144

Illinois Baking Company, 69

International Association of Ice Cream Manufacturers (IAICM), 42, 66, 67, 113, 115, 122, 150

"I-Scream Bar," 74

Jamaican Magic, 147

James II, King of England, 18

Japan, ice cream in, 36, 59

Jargon, soda jerking, 99–108

Jefferson, Thomas, recipe for ice cream, 24

Joe Lowe Corporation (Popsicle Industries), 83, 85

Johnson, Lyndon B., 59

Johnson, Nancy, 25–26

"Johnson Patent Ice-Cream Freezer," 27

"Johnson-Young" crank-and-paddle freezer, 27

Jones, Michael Owen, 102

Keeney, Philip G., 139

"Keep 'Em Buying to Keep 'Em Flying," 50

Kid Millions (film), 40

Knauer, Mrs. Virginia, 116–117

Korb, Harold, "U.S. Champion Soda Jerker," 174

Korean War, 45

Kosher ice cream, 124

Lafayette, Marquis de, 89

Laurie, Piper, 52

Lee, Ralph A., 74

Lemon Sherbet, 143

Let's Sell Ice Cream, 174–175, 181

Lincoln, Abraham, 31

"Linguistic Concoctions of the Soda Jerker," 102

Lippincott, John, 87

Lipton, Thomas J., Inc., 83

Liquid Carbonic Company, 155

Loft's candy stores, 13

Look magazine, 6, 8–9

Lost Men of American History, 64

Louis Sherry ice cream, 9

Low-Fat Vanilla Ice Milk, 132

"Lucky Sticks" case, 83

"Lunar Cheesecake" ice cream, 58

Index

McNamara, Robert, 46

Madison, Dolley, 24

"Make Mine Vanilla," 175–176

Making Good with Good Humor (manual), 81

Mallowberry, 146

Malted, 60, 187–188

Manuals, soda jerk, 97, 99

Maple Parfait, 152

Maple Temptation Sauce, 159

Marchiony, Italo, 67, 68

Marchiony-Hamwi row, 68, 69

Mary Browne Sundae, 159

Maryland, University of, Dept. of Dairy Science at, 123

Matthews, John, 85, 86, 89

Mattus, Reuben, 57

Mecla (frozen dessert), 16

de Medicis, Catherine, 17

Meehan, Michael J., 179

Mellow-Cream Chocolate Soda—1946, 174

Mencken, H. L., 94, 102

Mikoyan, Anastas, 52

Milk Industry Foundation, 113

"Milk in Its Finest Form," 51

Milk shake, 188

Miller's ice cream parlors (Michigan), 6

Missouri Cone Company, 70

Molds, ice cream, where to buy, 193

Montagu, Lady Mary Wortley, 20

"Moon Shot," 59

Morale, ice cream and, 44–46

"Morale food," 44

Mt. McKinley Ice Cream Company (Fairbanks, Alaska), 56

National Biscuit Company, 70

National Dairy Council, 10, 65, 145

National Geographic magazine, 67, 70

National Soda Fountain Guide, 155–156

Nation's Restaurant News, The, 8

Nelson, Christian, 73–74, 76, 77, 85

New York magazine, 4, 9, 111

New York Stock Exchange, 36

New York *Times,* The, 6, 9, 45, 48, 49, 59, 67, 68, 172

Nixon, Richard M., 58

North, Robert, 115, 122

North Pole Sundae, 157

O'Conor, Herbert R., 52, 53

O'Hare, George, 97

Ohio State University, Dept of Dairy Technology, 123

"Operation Deep Freeze," 46

Ozark ice cream, 35

Palmer, Carl J., 61

Panama Cooler, 154

Paramount Pictures, 42

Patents for ice cream inventions, 25–26, 74, 76, 77, 81, 83, 95

Peanut Malted, 162

Petersen's (Chicago), 10

Philadelphia Vanilla Ice Cream, 133

Physick, Dr. Phillip S., 87

La Physiologie du Goût, 22

"Pickles and Ice Cream," 141

Plain Vanilla Ice Cream, 134

Plaza Hotel, ice cream parlor in, 4

Polo, Marco, 17
Popsicle, 57, 73, 83
"Pot freezer method," 24–25
Praline, 146
"Precise" Chocolate Malted Milk, 167
Priestley, Joseph, 85, 86
Prohibition, effect of on ice cream
    sales, 34–35, 38–39, 94
Puffer, A. D., 87
Puller, General Lewis B., "Chesty,"
    45

Queen Ann Sundae, 158

Radio, ice cream mentioned on, 81
Rainbow Parfait, 182
Refrigerator Ice Cream (Peanut But-
    ter)—1943, 172–173
Reuben, Dr. David, 9–10
Reynolds, R. S., 76
Reynolds Metals, 76
Riordan, John Lancaster, 102
Robbins, Irv, 124, 125
Robinson, Francis J., 22
Robinson's Drugstore (Dayton, Ten-
    nessee), 92, 94
Rogers, Ginger, 40
Roosevelt, Franklin D., 42
Russell Stover Candy Stores, 76
Roussel, Eugene, 89, 91

Saga of the Ice Cream Cone, The, 68
St. Louis Exposition (Fair)—1904,
    66–69

Schlink, F. J., 120
Schrafft's, 58
Schuette, H. A., 22
Schwab's Drugstore (Hollywood and
    Vine), 42
Scoops, where to buy, 194–195
Scopes, John Thomas, 92
Scopes trial, 92, 94
Sealtest ice cream, 57, 59
Seltzer, 87, 91
Sensuous Woman, The, 9
Sherbets and ices, **141**
"Shotgun Menu Mistake, The," 54
Silliman, Benjamin, 87
Snow, as dessert, 17
Soda Fountain Beverages, 63
"Soda Fountain Lingo," 102
Soda Fountain magazine, 94, 97, 99,
    158, 159, 161, 164
Soda Fountain Manufacturers Asso-
    ciation, 61, 96
"Soda-Fountain, Restaurant and Tav-
    ern Calls," 102
Soda fountains, 33, 36, 42, 43, 53, 57,
    58, 63, 85
  history, 86–108
  where to buy, 195
Soda jerking
  tips, 187
  tools, 149–150
Soda jerks, 34, 96–108, 188
  tips for, 188
Soda water, 150
*Soda Water Guide and Book of Tested
    Recipes,* 155
Sour Cream Sauce, 146
Spatula Soda Water Guide, 97, 156

Spitzer, Silas, 175
Stickney, Mrs. Anita, 119
Stover, Russell, 74, 76
Strawberry Mousse, 179
Strawberry Thickshake—1971, 185
Sullivan, Stephen H., 67, 70
"Sundae Schools," 43
"Sundae Specials," 66
"Sunday Soda Menace," 65
"Super ice creams," 51
"Survey of Frozen Dessert Trends,"
    120
Sweden, ice cream in, 59
"Sweethearts of the Ice Cream Indus-
    try," 52
Sweet Potato Ice Cream, 140–141
Swensen's (San Francisco area), 6, 12
Syrups and toppings, 91, 140, 144–
    145
  tips for use of, 187

Taylor, C. L., 97
Third Degree, 161
Thirty Seconds Over Tokyo, 47
Tips, making and serving ice cream,
    185–188
Tortoni, 20
Triple Ice Cream Bombe with Fluffy
    Chocolate-Nut Sauce, 178–179
Tufts, James W., 63
Tune-In Sundae, 161
Twin Popsicle, 85

United States Department of Agricul-
    ture, 33, 37, 128, 141

United States Department of Com-
    merce, 36
United States Foil Company, 76
United States Patent Office, 72, 77
Up to Date (newsletter), 113
Union of Soviet Socialist Republics,
    ice cream in, 52

Vanilla Custard Ice Cream, 134
Vanilla Poached Eggs on Toast, 165
Veterans of Foreign Wars, 45
"Victory Sundaes," 50
Vienna, ice cream in, 20
Vietnam War, 45
da Vinci, Leonardo, 72

Waldorf Astoria Hotel, 97, 166
Waldorf Parfait, 167
Walgreen's Drugstores, 102, 163
Wall Street, 3, 79
Walnut Cream Syrup, 153–154
Warhol, Andy, 58
"Warhol Sundae," 58
Washington Monument Sundae, 174–
    175
Water, carbonated, 86–87, 89, 91
  test for, 187
Washington, George, 22, 24
Wayne, Major General "Mad" An-
    thony, 44
Western Ice Cream News, The, 68
Whelan's Drugstores, 102
White, E. F., 97, 156
White's Flyer, 155

"Who's Who in the Soda Fountain World," 97

Wildes, Harry Emerson, 44

Wilson, Woodrow, 74

Wil Wright's (Los Angeles), 10

Wisconsin, University of, Laboratory of Foods and Sanitation at, 22

Women's Christian Temperance Union, 45, 65

"World's Fair Cornucopia," 66–67, 69

World War I, ice cream in, 44–45

World War II, ice cream in, 43, 46–50, 59, 63

Young, William G., 27

Zalabia (Persian pastry), 66

Paul Dickson

Paul Dickson is a free-lance writer who spent a portion of his high school years as a soda jerker. Despite intervening activities, his interest in ice cream remains as keen as it was during those lazy 1950s afternoons when he slung a mean No. 24 scoop. Mr. Dickson was born in Yonkers, New York, in 1939, was graduated from Wesleyan University, and served in the navy. He has published articles in such publications as *Esquire, Saturday Review, The Nation, Washington Monthly,* the Washington *Post,* and *The Progressive.* Together with his wife, Nancy, he lives in Washington, D.C., a good but (unlike Philadelphia) not a great ice cream town.